WHY CUSTOMERS NOW RUN COMPANIES—AND HOW TO PROFIT FROM IT

THE BRAND FLIP

THE BRAND

A WHITEBOARD OVERVIEW BY **MARTY NEUMEIER**

THE BRAND FLIP

WHY CUSTOMERS NOW RUN COMPANIES—AND HOW TO PROFIT FROM IT

A WHITEBOARD OVERVIEW BY MARTY NEUMEIER

NEW RIDERS

FIND US ON THE WEB AT: WWW.NEWRIDERS.COM
NEW RIDERS IS AN IMPRINT OF PEACHPIT, A DIVISION OF PEARSON EDUCATION
TO REPORT ERRORS, PLEASE SEND A NOTE TO ERRATA@PEACHPIT.COM

ACQUISITIONS EDITOR	**PRODUCTION EDITOR**	**DESIGN DIRECTOR**
NIKKI ECHLER MCDONALD	DAVID VAN NESS	MARTY NEUMEIER

PROOFREADER	**INDEXER**	**DESIGNER**
LIZ WELCH	REBECCA PLUNKETT	IRENE HOFFMAN

ISBN 13: 978-0-134-17281-1
ISBN 10: 0-134-17281-7

7 2021

PRINTED AND BOUND IN THE UNITED STATES OF AMERICA

TO MY TRIBE

PREFACE

You hold in your hand a book. But what is a book? Is it something you BUY or something you BECOME? To many authors and publishers, a book is 75,000 words on 300 pages held between two rigid covers that measure 6 by 9 inches. Or, it's 75,000 electronic words that can be resized, customized, read, and annotated by the user.

Every book is both container and content. The container is what gets made, advertised, sold, and distributed. If it looks like a book, feels like a book, and downloads like a book, it must be a book.

But what about the content? What if some people view a business book not as a trophy on their bookshelf but as a step change in their career? What if some people—and here I mean you—want the most inspiration in the least number of hours?

In that case, a book needs to have the least number of words, not the most. It should be designed to stay in your mind, not in your hand. It should get you out from the covers and into your projects as fast as possible. And it should reveal its deeper wisdom reading after reading. This is the book I tried to write. It'll require two hours of your valuable time, which I don't take lightly. But if it's the book you need, it'll pay you back for years.

—Marty Neumeier

CONTENTS

INTRODUCTION   **1**

10 NEW REALITIES   **8**

PART 1

FLIPPING THE BRAND

PRODUCTS →◦→ MEANING   **19**

TANGIBLE →◦→ IMMATERIAL   **24**

SELLING →◦→ ENROLLING   **28**

COMPANY IDENTITY →◦→ CUSTOMER IDENTITY   **32**

BETTER PRODUCTS →◦→ BETTER CUSTOMERS   **36**

CUSTOMER SEGMENTS →◦→ CUSTOMER TRIBES   **40**

TRANSACTIONS →◦→ RELATIONSHIPS   **46**

PART 2

LEADING THE TRIBE

AUTHORITY →◦→ AUTHENTICITY   **51**

COMPETING →◦→ DIFFERENTIATING   **57**

PROCESSES →◦→ VALUES   **62**

FEATURES →◦→ EXPERIENCES   **68**

PUNISHMENT →◦→ PROTECTION   **77**

PART 3

DESIGNING THE WAY FORWARD

DECIDING →◦→ DESIGNING   **85**

PLANS →◦→ EXPERIMENTS   **92**

OVERCHOICE →◦→ SIMPLICITY   **100**

STATIC BRANDS →◦→ LIQUID BRANDS   **104**

STORYTELLING →◦→ STORYFRAMING   **114**

PURCHASE FUNNEL →◦→ BRAND LADDER   **120**

TAKE-HOME LESSONS   **131**

RECOMMENDED READING   **134**

ACKNOWLEDGMENTS   **136**

INDEX   **139**

NOTES   **145**

ABOUT THE AUTHOR   **146**

THOSE WHO INITIATE CHANGE WILL HAVE A BETTER OPPORTUNITY

TO MANAGE THE CHANGE THAT IS INEVITABLE. —WILLIAM POLLARD

INTRODUCTION

One of the more stunning insights in the theory of management came from Peter Drucker, a practical visionary who changed business discourse with his 1973 book THE PRACTICE OF MANAGEMENT. He said that a business has only one valid purpose: to create a customer.

What's more, he said, if the purpose of a business is to create a customer, then it has only two basic functions—innovation and marketing. Innovation produces the products, and marketing tells the stories that sell them. These two activities drive results, and all the others are costs.

Drucker was ahead of his time. The discipline of branding had been stuck in the Industrial Age, and lacked strategic subtlety. He couldn't have known that someday it would gather up the very concerns he was talking about—innovation, marketing, and the primacy of customers—into a toolbox of principles that could be studied, practiced, and improved over time. Or that the word BRAND itself would become shorthand for the Drucker way of thinking.

Thirteen years ago I tried to redefine branding in my book THE BRAND GAP, and took it further in my next book ZAG. As of this writing, THE BRAND

GAP'S principles have been viewed online by more than 10 million people, and ZAG has been named one of the top 100 business books of all time. These volumes have stayed relevant, and continue to form the basis of my work.

Then why write another book? Because the rapid advance of technology, rather than making THE BRAND GAP and ZAG seem dated, has made them seem timid. For me, they occupy the odd position of being visionary and incomplete at the same time. In my world of workshops and keynotes, they've ceased to scratch the itch.

When I wrote THE BRAND GAP, the term SOCIAL MEDIA wasn't in popular use. Neither were VIRAL, SMARTPHONE, TABLET, DISRUPTION, TRANSPARENCY, and SELFIE. Back then the central problem of branding was how to align business strategy with customer experience. Today it's how to empower the customers who will drive your success.

"We believe putting customers first is the only way to create lasting value for shareholders," said Amazon CFO Tom Szkutak. Amazon is

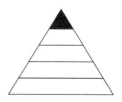

one of a growing number of companies that have adapted to—and encouraged—the primacy of customers.

To the degree that the customer is boss, shouldn't we know what the boss wants? The best customers are no longer consumers or market segments or tiny blips in big data. They're individuals with hopes, dreams, needs, and emotions. They exercise judgment, indulge in whims, express personal views, and write their own life stories. They're proactive, skeptical, and creative. They've reached the top of Maslow's Pyramid, where the goals are autonomy, growth, and fulfillment. They don't "consume." HAVING more runs a distant second to BEING more.

An explosion of connectivity, and the power it gives customers, is turning companies upside down. The question isn't WHETHER your industry will be disrupted, but WHEN. Companies today have a stark choice: they can leap into future and possibly land on their feet, or they can wait for roiling disruption to upend them.

This is the challenge of the brand flip.

To better understand what has changed in brand building, it might help to look at old and new

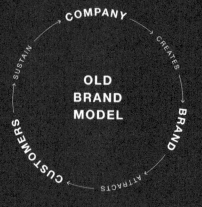

OLD BRAND MODEL

COMPANY · CREATES · BRAND · ATTRACTS · CUSTOMERS · SUSTAIN

NEW BRAND MODEL

COMPANY · CREATES · CUSTOMERS · BUILD · BRAND · SUSTAINS

diagrams on the left page. The old model of brand was based on the logic of factory management. The company created the brand (through products and advertising), the brand attracted customers (as a captive audience), and customers supported the company (through repeat purchases).

The new model of brand is similar, but with one important difference: the order of events. Instead of creating the brand first, the company creates customers (through products and social media), then the customers create the brand (through purchases and advocacy), and the brand sustains the company (through customer loyalty). This model takes into account a profound and counterintuitive truth: a brand is not owned by the company, but by the customers who draw meaning from it. Your brand isn't what YOU say it is. It's what THEY say it is.

In the pre-flip days, a company could find a hole in the market, fill it with a product, determine a price, and drive the product into people's lives with heavy advertising and distribution. The only choice customers had was to buy or not to buy. The real power lay with the company and its leaders, who were seen as authority figures.

Today's customers reject that authority, and at

the same time require a measure of control over the products they love. They no longer BUY brands. They JOIN brands. They want a vote in what gets produced and how it gets delivered. They're willing to roll up their sleeves and help out, not only by promoting the brand to their friends, but by contributing content, volunteering ideas, and even selling products or services. Many of them know more about the company, its products, its pricing, and its competitors than the CEO and employees do. In a very real sense, the best customers are co-leading companies into the post-flip world.

Each of the 18 chapters describes a single flip—an accepted business "truth" upended by technological change. These individual flips add up to the overall flip. Yet this book is not just a description of change, but a prescription for it. At the center is a simple matrix for modeling the relationship between your company and its customers. To demonstrate the matrix, I've added the example of a hypothetical tea company— a modest startup that would surely languish in obscurity under the old model of branding.

But what would happen if we flipped it?

1

Power has shifted from companies to *customers*

2

People are not focused on products, but *meaning*

3

Customers buy products to build their *identities*

4

They hate being sold, but they love to *buy*

5

They buy in *tribes* to feel safe and successful

6

The battle is no longer between companies, but *tribes*

7

The company with the strongest tribe *wins*

8
Tribes are connected through *technology*

9

Brands need to *flow* through multiple technologies

10

The most successful brands are not static, but *fluid*

PART 1 : FLIPPING THE BRAND

If you could take a time machine back to the late 19th century, you would see a world full of advertising pitches that would seem quaint by today's standards. You'd certainly find heroic attempts to differentiate OUR product from THEIR product, but the difference would be based mostly on the product's FEATURES. This was a marketplace of tangible goods for functional needs.

However, if you eased the time machine forward a few decades, say, to 1925, you'd notice that marketers had begun to step up their game. They realized that features weren't at the heart of what customers really wanted. What they wanted were the BENEFITS that those features delivered. Smart marketers began to focus on functional benefits.

Go ahead. Push the stick ahead another 50 years. It's 1975, and marketers are looking for the next big advantage. A few visionaries have located a higher point of leverage—the differentiated EXPERIENCE. "The experience of using OUR product," they seemed to say, is better than "the experience of using THEIR product."

Today's marketers are fully invested in customer experience. They still talk about features and benefits, but experience has become the goal, the game, and the playing field.

Did you notice, in the course of your journey through time, how marketing has changed? It moved from what the product has, to what it does, to how it makes people feel. It started out with an object created in a factory and ended up with an emotion created in a customer. It went from totally within the company's control to partially outside it.

And this trend hasn't stopped. Today's customers want more than products, more than features, more than benefits, even more than experiences. They want MEANING. They want a sense of BELONGING. They want creative CONTROL over their life stories. And they're likely to assemble those stories from all the elements they find around them, including products, services, and brands. "If I buy this product," they seem to say, "what does that make me?" Now you can bring the time machine to a stop. We've arrived back where we started, at the dawn of the "meaning economy."

At this point I'd like to establish a working definition of brand, if only for the purpose of the book. Otherwise we might easily jump the rails with so many definitions of brand littering the tracks. I count six or seven common ones. Let's start with the least helpful, and work our way to the most helpful.

A LOGO. We can dispense with this definition quickly. A logo is not a brand—it's only a symbol for a brand. A brand is much more than a logo. I remember leading a presentation in which the CEO pointed to a packaging mockup and asked, "Can we make the brand bigger?" I said we couldn't, but we could certainly make the logo bigger. A bigger brand was not in the budget.

A PRODUCT. People often refer to products as brands, and I understand why. It's shorthand for "branded product" or "branded service." But for the sake of conceptual clarity, let's keep products and services separate from brands. A brand is much more than a product or service.

THE SUM OF ALL IMPRESSIONS. This is sloppy thinking. If we were to add up all the impressions and experiences associated with a product or service and draw a line under them, the sum would still be just a lot of impressions and experiences. What do you do with that information? How does it lead to smarter brand decisions?

A PROMISE. A brand certainly implies a promise

to customers, a guarantee of minimum performance, or a certain level of satisfaction. Every company should know what its brand is promising to its customers. And the company should never over-promise just to make a sale. However, a promise is only a component of a brand, not the brand itself.

A RELATIONSHIP. It's quite true that a brand is a relationship between a company and its customers. In fact, a large part of this book is based on that understanding. But as a definition, will it really help? If I understand that marriage is a relationship, does it make me a better husband? If I believe I have a rela-tionship with the government, will I become a better citizen? Okay, a brand is a relationship. So what?

A REPUTATION. This definition seems almost perfect. Once you conceive of a brand as a reputation, you can think more clearly about how to build it, shape it, and protect it. It's a lot like a personal reputation. Except that a personal reputation is something you can affect personally, whereas a commercial reputation requires the coordinated effort of many people with differing views and skills. How do we build it? Who is it for? What does it mean? The definition doesn't say.

A CUSTOMER'S GUT FEELING ABOUT A PRODUCT, SERVICE, OR COMPANY. Are we there yet? Well, let's see. It puts the customer in the center of the picture. It focuses everyone in the company on customer perceptions—those fleeting experiences and fickle emotions that determine meaning. And it offers a simple way to measure progress. If we listen to what customers say, and watch what they do, we can find out where we stand with them. Yes! I think we might be there.

Now that we have a basic definition to go forward with, where shall we head next? Let's move on to the second flip—how people and technology are favoring non-material goods over tangible goods.

WHAT IS A LOGO WORTH?

A logo is not a brand. But is it valuable? Probably more than most companies realize. A logo (let's call it a combination of a name and graphic treatment) has the ability to compress the purpose, personality, and uniqueness of a brand into an elegant, meaningful symbol. This symbol, if conceived well, can be unpacked by customers in ways that are hugely valuable to the company over many years.

How much should the company pay for a logo? About as much as a car, as it turns out. Think about the logo as a company car for brand meaning. You can buy a car for $500. It may be an eyesore, but it'll get you from A to B if you're lucky. At the other end of the spectrum, you could pay up to $500,000 for a uniquely designed beauty with impeccable engineering. It'll strike awe into the hearts of onlookers, and perform well for a good 25 years or more. Realistically, however, the right symbol for most companies will be in the $20,000 to $75,000 range, depending on their prospects. Is your brand symbol worth the price of a car? What kind?

TANGIBLE ↝ IMMATERIAL

In my family, holiday presents are shrinking. Maybe you've noticed the same thing in yours. We used to buy each other presents like sweaters, books, toys, bath soap, and perfume. Now we buy gift cards—for clothing, media, gadgets, spa days, and charitable donations. All that awaits beneath the tree is a thin layer of envelopes. What gives?

We're not being lazy. We know instinctively that, while sweaters and books deliver great experiences, the pleasure of a gift can be doubled if we add another experience on top of it—the intangible bonus of shopping, choosing, or having more control. As Liquid Agency chief creative officer Alfredo Muccino puts it, technology has flipped our mindset from "I need stuff" to "I want an experience."

Beneath this trend, industry is undergoing a massive migration from a material-based economy to a digital one. We're removing paper from books, polycarbonate from music, and physical shelving from stores. Many people would now rather travel than own a home. Some are ditching their cars in favor of services like Zipcar and Uber. And when cars start driving themselves, who will want a garage when we can just whistle for our rides?

In his thought-provoking book WHAT TECHNO-LOGY WANTS, Kevin Kelly points out that in the past six years the average weight per dollar of U.S exports had fallen by half. "We are steadily substituting intangible design, flexibility, innovation, and smartness for rigid, heavy atoms," he says.

This was foreseen by Alvin Toffler in his 1991 book POWERSHIFT. He predicted that the power of immaterial value would extend even to money, calling it nearly a "religious conversion" from "a trust in permanent, tangible things like gold or paper to a belief that even the most intangible, ephemeral electronic blips can be swapped for goods and services. Our wealth," he said, "is a wealth of symbols." Both our money and our goods are becoming intangible.

A recent study of the S&P 500 showed that the monetary value of intangible assets had increased from 17 percent to 80 percent over a 30-year period. The largest of these company assets were brands. What has driven the increase is an improved ability to connect emotionally with customers through qualities such as immediacy,

25 INTANGIBLES THAT ADD VALUE

AUTHENTICITY	Offer the real thing
AVAILABILITY	Make it easy to get anywhere, anytime
BELONGING	Offer a sense of community
CLARITY	Make it very easy to understand
CERTAINTY	Remove all doubt about its benefits
CONTROL	Put the customer in charge
CURATION	Act as tastemaker on behalf of customers
DELIGHT	Deliver more than reliability
FINDABILITY	Make it easy to see, choose, or discover
FLEXIBILITY	Be eager to accommodate requests
GUIDANCE	Add support, learning, or interpretation
HOPE	Offer a chance at future success
IMMEDIACY	Give quick delivery or priority access
INCLUSIVENESS	Allow customers to contribute
LIGHTNESS	Eliminate weight or density
OPTIMISM	Make customers feel positive
PATRONAGE	Help customers support a cause
PERSONALIZATION	Let customers configure their purchases
PROTECTION	Keep customers safe from extra costs
SAFETY	Protect customers from physical harm
SIMPLICITY	Streamline the product or purchase
SPEED	Help customers save time
STYLE	Incorporate beauty or personality
SURPRISE	Disrupt expectations
SYMBOLISM	Help build customers' identities

personalization, self-identity, and empowerment.

Until we can purchase essentials like food, shelter, clothing, and machines as software code, we'll need our industries to produce tangible goods. The goods themselves may be commodities, but the intangible benefits wrapped around them will make them unique and empowering.

A recent study shows that three-quarters of customers think companies should work to improve the quality of their lives. Only one-quarter believe that companies are succeeding. There's plenty of room at the top.

Remember our definition? A brand is a customer's gut feeling about a product, service, or company. But there's more. A successful brand can become a touchstone in a customer's life— a vivid symbol of what's useful, delightful, and even magical. When a product becomes a symbol, the symbol becomes the product. It can offer tremendous value as a building block in a customer's personal identity.

My wife and I once spent a week in Istanbul, immersing ourselves in the sights, sounds, and spicy aromas of the ancient city. If we had been dressed in American flags we couldn't have been more obvious to the tourist vendors.

"You want buy rug? Best rugs in Instanbul!"

At every shop we passed, a vendor would rush out with a well-worn hook line: "I love America! Best deal for you today!"

The stall owners in the Grand Bazaar have one mantra: CLOSE THIS SALE. They have no insight into customer desires. No interest in future business. No fear of reprisals from disgruntled buyers. What they have is an endless parade of wide-eyed newbies passing through their souq. They will never see these two Americans again. It's now or never.

The business culture in the old city is a culture of SALES. It's about as far as you can get from branding. And what's sad is that it doesn't work very well. The shop owners are playing a constant game of catch-up with their costs, engaged in a daily struggle to sell the same goods that every other shop owner sells.

Branding takes a different approach. It assumes that customers are more valuable over time than as one-off transactions. It considers that they will pay more for a unique product than a generic one. And it understands that customers have aspirations beyond getting a low price on this particular product or service. Companies may SELL products. But customers JOIN brands. They sign up with companies that see them as people, and avoid companies that see them as targets.

Traditional marketing leans more toward selling than branding. While it appreciates the halo that branding brings to sales, it focuses more on short-term results than long-term growth. This bird-in-the-hand approach is still the default position for most companies today. After all, without sales THIS QUARTER there may be no NEXT QUARTER. The result is a more tactical role for marketing managers, rather than the strategic one they enjoyed when advertising was king. Yet selling, whether through personal sales or advertising, can only boost revenues for one or two quarters. Branding creates a flywheel effect that can drive success for decades. It creates a company's most powerful strategic advantage: customer loyalty.

THE AIM OF MARKETING IS TO MAKE SELLING SUPERFLUOUS.

For marketing managers who aspire to climb the strategic ladder, expertise in branding is the ticket out of the tactical. The high cost of selling is really a tax on bad branding. Anything you can do to lower that tax is a strategic win. As Peter Drucker put it, "The aim of marketing is to make selling superfluous."

A few years back Toyota got its brand in trouble. The company had forgotten the reason its revenues were so robust—the strength of its brand and the quality it promised. When the cars failed, the brand crashed. Akio Toyoda blamed the whole fiasco on sales gone wild: "Some people just got too big-headed," he said. "They focused too excessively on profit." What he meant was SHORT-TERM profit, not the long-term profit that comes from brand loyalty.

The numbers on the opposite page would mean little to a vendor at the Grand Bazaar. But they make a strong case for building a business on customer RETENTION rather than customer ACQUISITION. Any effort to get customers is market-ing. Any effort to get customers and KEEP THEM is branding. For companies with vision, branding is the more strategic path.

THE POWER OF LOYALTY

The most loyal 50 percent of customers would pay a 25 percent premium before switching brands.

Loyal customers spend 33 percent more than new customers.

The probability of selling to a new customer is only 5–20 percent, whereas the probability of selling to an existing customer is 60–70 percent.

Customers who have an emotional connection to a company are 4 times as likely to do business with it.

In many categories, the most loyal 10 percent of customers generates 50 percent of the revenues.

In some sectors, a 2 percent increase in loyalty is equivalent to a 10 percent cost reduction.

A 5 percent increase in customer retention can mean a 30 percent increase in profits.

A 5 percent increase in loyalty can mean a 95 percent increase in profits over a customer's lifetime.

COMPANY IDENTITY ↝ CUSTOMER IDENTITY

In the mid-20th century when IBM, CBS, RJR, and other initials ruled the roost, a service business grew up around identity design. At the time, a brand was literally a brand—a typographical hot poker used to burn an identifying mark onto the company's products and, with enough repetition, into customers' minds. The focus was on "who we are," making sure that WE looked modern, organized, and professional. The prize went to the identities that pleased the most eyes. The best brandmarks were beautiful, and still are.

Business in those days was so company-centric that customers were treated as cattle, commercial herds to be fenced, fed, and harvested for corporate sustenance. I'm exaggerating, but consider the phrases we still use to describe marketing: we segment audiences, target customers, round up leads, and capture market share. A business with herd-like customers is called a cash cow, and people are called consumers, as if their only job is to graze on the prairie until they can be segmented, targeted, and converted into cash.

In the new customer-centric marketplace, the shoe is on the other hoof. "Who we are" is much less important than "who THEY are." CUSTOMER identity, not COMPANY identity, is the secret to building a flipped brand. It's not enough to find out who your customers are. You need to help them become the people they want to be. Their identity is shaped with every choice they make, with every product they buy.

Now we come to the essence of the flip: If the goal is to create customers, as Peter Drucker suggested, shouldn't we also be designing them? I don't mean this in some Big Brother, Frankenstein sort of way. I mean, shouldn't we be designing a FRAMEWORK in which our customers can see themselves, build their unique identities, and ultimately become who they are? My own observation is that creating anything without design is usually a mess. The last thing anyone wants is a messy business.

Let's pursue this line of thinking with a hypothetical example.

Imagine this: On a recent trip to Guatemala, an entrepreneur named Lori learns that the Mayans had a practice of making tea from the discarded husks of cacao beans. They simply poured hot water over the husks and added a little honey. She tried it herself and VOILÀ!—

a natural chocolate drink that, when sweetened with stevia instead of honey, is not only delicious but calorie-free. What's more, the cacao industry views the husks as a waste product, making them cheaper to source than coffee beans or tea leaves.

Slowly, the idea for a new beverage company grows in her mind.

What should she do next? There's nothing inherently ownable about the idea of chocolate tea. Anyone could copy it, and someone prob- ably will. She realizes her best bet is to develop a highly focused brand—a brand for customers who love both chocolate and tea, of course, but what else? Her research shows that the most avid fans of chocolate and tea are women. But which women? Where are they? What are their goals?

More important, who do they want to become?

Anyone could have predicted that an Airbnb, Etsy, Zipcar, or Kickstarter might be essential to someone's life. And it's not hard to understand how trend-riders like Whole Foods, Method, and Patagonia could attract millions of passionate customers. But is it possible for a "nothing" product like chocolate tea to build that kind of following?

Google founder Larry Page had a simple goal: to make people a little smarter. Steve Jobs's goal at Apple was to make them a little more creative. Mini USA wants its customers to be conscientious drivers. And Joie de Vivre founder Chip Conley wanted his hotel guests to "refresh their identities." What should Lori want for her customers? How might she help women build their identities?

She decides to focus on women with children, like herself—smart, busy mothers whose identities can often get lost in the shuffle, especially without "me time" and personal rituals to keep them grounded. She begins reading books on psychology and selfhood. "The self is a fragile construction," said psychologist Mihaly Csikszentmihalyi. "Without external props it can fade and go out of focus."

Lori sees her opening.

BETTER PRODUCTS ↗ BETTER CUSTOMERS

Ambitious companies are eager to invest in innovative products. They seek to create new features, new solutions, new markets, new industries. Ideally, they want to invent a product or service that disrupts the existing ecosystem, redefines their category, and generates monopoly profits for decades. They're barking up the wrong tree.

In a flipped business, the product is not the innovation, the CUSTOMER is. The battle is no longer between companies, but between the people who buy from them. In other words, the nature of your customers determines the future of your company. The company with the best customers wins.

You can see this principle at work in the trajectory of Apple. From early on, the company invested heavily in its customers, making technology accessible to non-techies, standing as a bulwark against lumbering giants such as IBM, giving computers to schoolchildren to inculcate a new kind of literacy. Even as Apple's market share slipped to 3 percent after the ouster of Steve Jobs, its customers remained passionate and vocal. When Jobs returned, he was joined by a talented army of volunteers who were eager to be led.

The lesson is this: Instead of thinking about how to improve and position your products, think about how to improve and position your customers. They're the ones who will fight for your success. In his book WHO DO YOU WANT YOUR CUSTOMERS TO BECOME?, Michael Schrage says, "Truly successful innovations generate wealth for their users, not just their creators." Wealth is not only financial. It can be social, educational, physical, spiritual, and temporal—any good that people get out of a product or service.

What's the highest good you can want for your customer?

Ritz-Carlton wants its guests to be more sophisticated. Its motto? "We are ladies and gentlemen serving ladies and gentlemen." When you treat yourself to the impeccable service at the Ritz, your self-image soars to lofty new heights, and you somehow find yourself exuding greater confidence, generosity, and charm.

Dell wants to "enable customers everywhere to grow, thrive, and reach their full potential." The company backs this up with its "nurture" program (which also generates order amounts of 25 percent higher than the previous average).

The primary good that a company can offer its customers is empowerment. The best brand builders see greatness in their customers, and figure out ways to enable it.

P&G puts its customers' ambitions right smack in its purpose statement: "We will provide branded products and services of superior quality and value that improve the lives of the world's customers, now and for generations to come."

By contrast, Las Vegas casinos care little about their customers' lives beyond offering a brief respite from the daily tedium. When visitors get back home, they'll face the same old grind, but with thinner wallets. This is the opposite of seeing greatness in customers. Instead, they see only weakness, naïveté, and addictive behavior.

Lori, meanwhile, comes to the realization that all profitable brands are habit-forming at some level. That's what makes them sustainable. The only question is whether the habit, on balance, is a healthy or unhealthy one. Both chocolate and tea can be habit-forming, since they appeal to the pleasure centers of the brain. But her tea contains little that might be considered unhealthy: there are no sugars or artificial ingredients. On the contrary, it contains compounds that people might consider health-giving, such as procyanidins, known to reduce the risk of heart disease; more antioxidants than green tea and red wine; and theobromine, a milder stimulant than caffeine. The effect is a slight boost in serotonin levels for a happy, mellow mood. All in all, a healthy habit.

But what else could it be? What does a busy mom want that the tea could provide? Lori makes a quick list.

- Caffeine-free substitute for coffee
- Guilt-free substitute for sugar drinks
- Time-out treat during a busy day
- Social time with visiting friends
- After-school ritual for talk time with kids
- Family after-dinner beverage
- Political statement about re-use

These are some of the "jobs" that the product could do for busy moms. What are we addressing? A lack of time, health concerns, worries about her kids' schooling, a desire to create family memories, a need to maintain social ties, and a desire to improve the environment.

We'll let these ideas steep while we examine the next flip, the mental shift from segments to tribes.

CUSTOMER SEGMENTS ↝ CUSTOMER TRIBES

Segmentation is a handy strategy for targeting customers in an existing market. You identify a large market, then cut it up into smaller slices according to categories such as GEOGRAPHY (regions, countries, cities), DEMOGRAPHICS (age, gender, occupation, education, income), PSYCHO-GRAPHICS (activities, interests, opinions), BEHAVIOR (product usage, familiarity, loyalty), or BENEFIT PREFERENCE (one segment per preference). Then you target each chunk with a different offering. Divide and conquer.

But how do you segment a market that doesn't exist yet? Or a quickly changing market where customers are moving targets? Or a market in which every customer wants to be his or her own segment? You have to flip your thinking. Instead of division, you need multiplication. Start with a small market and scale it up with social media. MULTIPLY and conquer.

Among the magical innovations wrought by the Internet is our ability to form groups across boundaries—whether geographic, demographic, psychographic, or other-graphic. Social tools now allow RIDICULOUSLY EASY GROUP-FORMING, a term coined by Sébastien Pacquet. REGF makes a hash out of segmentation, since people routinely ignore the boundaries marketers place on them. We just go where we want to go, do what we want to do, and become who we want to become. We want to be unique, but we want to be unique in groups. We want to stand out, but we want to stand out together. In the age of easy group-forming, the basic unit of measurement is not the segment but the TRIBE.

A tribe is any group of people who share not only interests, but information. They talk to each other. They identify with their tribes: I'm a surfer. I'm an Anglophile. I'm a gamer. I'm a cat person. They also identify with brands: I'm an Audi person. I'm an Android person. I'm a Mets fan. I'm a Thronie. Since tribes can form quickly and organically, they're tailor-made for growing a brand.

A tribe is not just another type of segment. You don't target a tribe. You support it. Grow it. Partner with it. Organize it. Research shows that customers who interact socially with other customers in a brand community often develop an intense sense of loyalty, both to the brand and to each other. These are the people who are most likely to stand up and fight for your success.

The best question to ask any new-product marketer is not "What size is the market?" but "You and what army?" Leaders often spend too much time organizing their employees, and not enough time organizing their customers—the group with the real power. By empowering and growing the tribe, you increase its strength against competing brands, which in turn increases your ability to support the tribe. What makes a brand strong is the mutual commitment between companies and their customers.

How do you build a tribe? The trick isn't finding the biggest possible market. It's seeking out the truest possible fans. "Too many organizations care about numbers, not fans," writes Seth Godin in his book TRIBES. "What they're missing is the depth of commitment and interconnection that true fans deliver." What fans respect is generosity and bravery. A brave company is one that stands up for its customers. Difference, not sameness. Innovation, not pandering to the crowd.

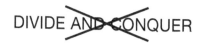

DIVIDE ~~AND CONQUER~~

MULTIPLY AND CONQUER

In a time when everyone is a potential media outlet, it's the true fans who can drive the conversation. But first they'll ask, "What does sharing this information say about me?" Next they'll ask, "Do I believe in the values of this company?" Every tribe has its social mores—its rules of behavior—a particular sense of what's right and what's wrong within the tribe. If you run afoul of these rules, you'll be shunned.

For example, back in the 1960s, a manufacturer invented a new surfboard that was stronger, lighter, and virtually "ding proof." This was exactly what surfers should have wanted. But the advertising made it obvious that the company was miles from any beach, and was blithely unaware of the heroes, history, and lingo of the sport. They were shut out by the tribe.

Tribes have insiders and outsiders. You can expand a tribe, but you can't break its rules. Knowing the rules—or helping define them from the beginning—is a prerequisite for leading the tribe.

Lori's potential market, women with children, is far too big to address with her modest product and limited budget. She needs to start smaller, find her true fans, and help them grow the brand from there. She decides to align with a vocal group of women who describe themselves as "mommy bloggers." Despite their self-deprecating name, mom bloggers are savvy, socially active, tech-smart women who either work outside the home or consider the home their main work. They have strong opinions about child rearing, education, health, and design. They share these opinions with followings that can be quite large.

The rules of the mom-blogging tribe vary, depending on which branch you look at. The branch that Lori seeks is mostly college-educated, food-conscious, and eco-concerned. They don't approve of Happy Meals or supersized drinks, and prefer to cook at home whenever they can. They care about the source of their ingredients, and often shop at Whole Foods or Trader Joe's. Since they're pressed for time, they buy quite a few products online. They're active in their kids' schools, and believe in volunteering in the community.

Using this insight, Lori works out the customer side of the brand equation. Let's take a look at what she has so far.

HEAD FOR
NEW IDEAS

EYE FOR
GOOD DESIGN

NOSE FOR
STORIES

TASTE FOR
NUTRITIOUS
FOOD

BROAD
SHOULDERS
FOR
COMMUNITY
WORK

SHARP
ELBOWS
FOR
PUSHING
BACK

SUPERIOR
BLOGGING
SKILLS

STRONG
LEGS FOR
RUNNING
ERRANDS

LONG
SHADOW
ONLINE

BOTH FEET
ON THE
GROUND

ANATOMY OF A MOM BLOGGER

TRANSACTIONS ⤳ RELATIONSHIPS

A sale requires a single transaction. A brand requires thousands or even millions of transactions, plus a huge number of relationships. To manage these relationships, you need to master the complex machinery of brand building. "Master" may be too strong a word, since no one can fully master such a creative, dynamic discipline. You'll occasionally get confused by all the cables, levers, meters, dials, and switches.

My advice? Keep it simple. Start with a document that maps out the basic contract between you and your customer. Then build it out element by element, move by move. With each new element or move, go back to the original contract and make sure you haven't violated its terms. If your brand effort gets off course (and it probably will), go right back to basics.

This brings me to the Brand Commitment Matrix, the simple tool at the heart of this book.

Here's how it works. Two columns, one for customers and one for the company. Each column contains three key statements. For customers, the statements will describe their IDENTITY (who they are), their AIMS (what they want), and their

tribe's MORES (how they belong).
These form the acronym IAM.

For the company, the statements will describe its PURPOSE (why we exist), its ONLYNESS (what we offer), and its VALUES (how we behave). These form the acronym POV.

The statements in each column should line up horizontally: customer identity and company purpose should align; customer aims and product "onlyness" should support each other; and tribal mores and company values should be in sync. If they don't align, what you have is a broken brand. If they do, you have the basis for a rich and productive relationship.

Let's use Lori's business idea to fill in the customer side of the matrix. In the IDENTITY space at the top, we'll take a stab at a customer vision. What does she want her customers to become?

"Busy mothers" who believe their contribution to their families and communities can resonate for generations sounds about right. But can chocolate tea accomplish such a lofty goal? We'll see.

Next, let's list the customer AIMS. These are the benefits that the product offers, from providing a coffee substitute to turning a waste product into a healthy habit. We should also address the other needs: time savings, healthy alternatives, school prioritization, family memories, social ties, and environmental concerns.

Finally, we'll list the rules, the MORES, of the mom-blogger tribe. These include a rejection of fast food, a family-first attitude, and a desire to collaborate with other moms through social media. They also include a high level of school involvement and a fair amount of community volunteering.

We've just completed the customer side of the Brand Commitment Matrix, a simple plan for partnership. This view of branding assumes the dawn of a "post-consumer world," in which the brand is the joint property of the company and the customer—the badge under which the customer builds her identity and creates her best self.

Now let's move over to the company side.

CUSTOMERS

IDENTITY

who they are

BUSY MOTHERS FOCUSED ON SERVING
NUTRITIOUS FOOD, EDUCATING THEIR
KIDS, CREATING GOOD FAMILY MEMORIES,
BUILDING STRONG SOCIAL TIES,
PROTECTING THE ENVIRONMENT, AND
CONTRIBUTING TO THE COMMUNITY

AIMS

what they want

- DELICIOUS EVERYDAY RITUAL
- CAFFEINE-FREE SUBSTITUTE FOR COFFEE
- NO-CAL SUBSTITUTE FOR SUGAR DRINKS
- AFTER-SCHOOL AND AFTER-DINNER TREAT
- ALCOHOL-FREE SOCIAL LUBRICANT
- POLITICAL STATEMENT FOR ENVIRONMENT
- EFFECTIVE FUNDRAISING PRODUCT
- PLATFORM FOR INFORMATION SHARING
- SYMBOL OF CARING PARENTHOOD

MORES

how they belong

- ARE TRIBAL BUT SELF-ASSURED
- OFTEN DISAGREE WITH MAJORITY VIEWS
- HAVE STRONG OPINIONS ON PARENTING
- BELIEVE IN THE POWER OF FAMILY
- WANT THEIR KIDS TO BE SELF-SUFFICIENT
- ARE OUTSPOKEN AND ARTICULATE
- AVOID FAST-FOOD RESTAURANTS
- TEND TO SHOP ONLINE
- CARE ABOUT THE SOURCE OF PRODUCTS
- ARE ACTIVE IN THEIR KIDS' SCHOOLING
- JOIN COMMUNITY ACTIVITIES

PART 2 : LEADING THE TRIBE

In 1984, millions of viewers watched spellbound as an athletic young woman ran up the aisle of a theater and hurled a sledgehammer at a colossal image of Big Brother. It was only a TV commercial for Apple, but it struck a chord with a consumer movement that was starting to flex its muscles.

The rise of consumerism, combined with the democratization of technology, encouraged us to look deeper inside the companies we do business with. People began to glimpse the motives, practices, and deceptions that had previously been obscured. Today, we no longer accept the authority of large organizations simply because they're large. We now look for something more than authority. We look for AUTHENTICITY.

We talk a lot about authenticity, but what is it? Honesty? Transparency? Reliability? Fairness? Folksiness? The closer we get to a definition, the more it seems like a mirage. What seems authentic to me might not be authentic to you. For example, I've always felt Madonna was rather inauthentic— a modestly talented musician corrupted by "material girl" ambitions. You may disagree, seeing Madonna as a self-created star with the courage to rebel—

perhaps like the hammer-thrower in the Apple commercial. Who's right? We both are. Authenticity is in the eye of the beholder.

To achieve authenticity with your tribe, you have to begin with PURPOSE. A company's purpose, simply stated, is the reason it's in business beyond making money. For example, Google's purpose is "to organize the world's information and make it universally accessible and useful." Apple's purpose is "to make tools for the mind." Cirque du Soleil's purpose is "to invoke the imagination, provoke the senses, and evoke the emotions." Coca-Cola's purpose is simplest of all: "To refresh the world."

Conversely, if your purpose is "to maximize shareholder value," you're aiming in the wrong direction. While shareholder value is a legitimate goal, it's not an authentic purpose. Your purpose should be aimed squarely at your customers, now and forever. You can change your mission, switch your market, shift your strategy, redesign your products, revise your taglines. But you should never change your purpose. It's the reason you exist— your true north.

When you align your purpose with your customer's identity, you get something called FIT.

FIT lets your customers know they've found the real deal, the genuine article, the honest-to-goodness-best-company-ever. To paraphrase author Virginia Postrel, they like it because they're LIKE it. Your purpose fits their identity.

Unfortunately, inauthenticity is rampant in the realm of traditional business. You only need to watch TV to see embarrassing examples of it. Maybe you've noticed Chevron's "We agree" campaign. The word "manipulation" doesn't begin to describe it. By pretending to support every worthwhile cause on the planet, fresh-faced actors in jeans try to distract viewers from the industry's ongoing record of irresponsibility. This comes off not so much as advertising as ham-handed propaganda. As one satirist said, "Chevron thinks 'denim' is short for 'environment.'"

The problem is that Chevron contradicts its stated goals. These include "to support universal human rights, protect the environment, and benefit the communities where we work." They then use advertising to cover up the shortfall. When a company perceived as inauthentic uses an inauthentic medium to deliver an inauthentic message, the only message people get is "We lie."

In contrast, many modern businesses skip advertising altogether and simply focus on being "remarkable," as Seth Godin puts it in his book PURPLE COW. Successful giants like IKEA, Starbucks, Apple, Whole Foods, and Amazon tend to focus more on customer experience than advertising. When they do use advertising, they use it to inform, not to deceive.

Smaller businesses are even less tempted by advertising. The boutique hotel chain Joie de Vivre bets most of its budget on the "identity refreshment" of its guests. Founder Chip Conley observed that the words a loyal customer would use to describe her dream product are "the same words she would use to describe herself."

Lifestyle retailer Anthropologie invests in "meaningful relationships" with customers. "Our customers are our friends, and what we do is never, ever, ever about selling to them," says president Glen Senk.

Shoe company Zappos spends far more on customer service than marketing. Its brand tribe includes not only customers but employees, who are encouraged to use their authentic voices in social media to help scale the brand community. A rare instance of Zappos "advertising" is a

THE AUTHENTICITY SCORECARD

Grade your company from 1–5 points on each item,
with 1 being "customers don't view us like this at all"
and 5 being "customers really do view us like this."

INAUTHENTIC	AUTHENTIC
___ Profits first	___ Profits + social good
___ Shareholder focus	___ Customer focus
___ Me-too products	___ Unique products
___ Fear of failure	___ Courage to innovate
___ Short-term focus	___ Long-term focus
___ Tangled business model	___ Simple business model
___ Overpaid leaders	___ Openness
___ Hard to work with	___ Easy to work with
___ Nickel-and-dime pricing	___ Relationship pricing
___ Hidden motives	___ Transparency
___ Advertising to persuade	___ Advertising to reveal
___ Loyalty programs	___ Organic loyalty
___ Continuous sales events	___ Surprise sales events
___ Legal hardball	___ Fair dealing
___ Robotic call centers	___ Real-time human help
___ Strict return policies	___ No questions asked
___ Fine-print contracts	___ Clear agreements
___ TOTAL POINTS	___ TOTAL POINTS

40-mile stretch of Adopt-a-Highway signs from the California border to its home in Nevada, in a public-spirited effort to keep the roadside clean.

In DECODING THE NEW CONSUMER MIND, marketing psychology professor Kit Yarrow lays out four qualities of an authentic company:

1. It cares and has the courage and confidence to listen without defensiveness.
2. It is sincere in showing its need and appreciation for its customers.
3. It is so clear about its integrity that it shows it openly and unashamedly.
4. It has a distinct personality and community.

She says that authenticity is potent because it's the "antidote to our online lives." We now inhabit a "photoshopped, intangible, and virtual online world" that causes us to crave what's real. In branding, what's real begins with purpose.

Lori has a strong sense of where her passion lies. She believes in the power of mothers to change the world. She knows that without attaching her product to a deeper meaning, it would end up just another alternative to Lipton or Tetley.

She writes on a slip of paper: "To create rituals that bring joy and health to families everywhere."

One reason purpose is so powerful is that it can help a company over hurdles that would seem insurmountable to less committed rivals. Others give up; you double down. Yet even purpose, passion, and commitment are not enough to win the race. You also need strategic differentiation.

Differentiation is the process of staking out a market position that you can own and defend. When your offering is unique and compelling enough, you don't need to compete on price. In fact, you don't need to compete much at all, except for attention. In most customers' minds there's only one Amazon, one Patagonia, one Dyson, one Twitter, one Muji, one Tesla, one Rosetta Stone, one Mayo Clinic. These companies and their products stand alone because of their design, their approach, their beliefs, their vision, or some other special quality. One way or another, they've achieved a state of ONLYNESS.

When you're the "only" in your category, you can name the tune that fast-following competitors must dance to. You can define the "criteria of purchase," according to Niraj Dawar, author of TILT. "You don't need to sweat every product launch, every new feature introduced by a competitor," he says. "Just pay attention to those who would wrest control of the criteria of purchase." For example, Volvo has famously differentiated on safety, allowing it to later take the credit for airbags and pedestrian detection. As long as Volvo stays focused on its onlyness, direct competitors will have to play second fiddle.

Onlyness allows you to start small by dominating a niche and growing it, or growing WITH it, over time. Multiply and conquer. Increase your dominance by giving your tribe the easily understood difference it needs to attract more like-minded customers. With the right differentiator, you can win a kind of monopoly, a significant competitive advantage in your category.

Peter Thiel, one of PayPal's founders, contends that this sort of monopoly is not a pathology or exception: "Monopoly is the condition of every successful business," he says. The idea is to avoid competition—or at least the direct kind that necessitates price cuts. When competitors engage in price wars, they compete away their profits. But how do you create onlyness? And how do you know if you already have it?

Here's a simple (but headache-producing) test. Complete the following sentence: "Our brand is the only _____ that _____." In the first blank, put the name of your category (robotics company, online university, fast-food chain). In the second blank put your key differentiator (sells voice-mimicking parrots, makes you the teacher, caters to vegans). When you compress your differentiator into a tiny statement, it's much easier to see what you have. Watch out for "ands" or commas—they're vampires that can drain away your difference.

Let's see how Lori might approach this task. Her chocolate tea has a few special factors built in: 1) the category itself is unique, or at least not well established; 2) the ingredients are organic and simple—cacao husks and stevia; 3) it has romantic roots in the Mayan culture; 4) it solves an environmental problem by turning a waste product into a useful one; and 5) its comforting chocolate taste appeals to children as well as adults.

These are indisputable facts, not empty marketing claims. They also sync up with the aims of Lori's customers, and could be touted as product benefits. But which one of these would make the most unique and compelling onlyness?

VIRGIN IS THE **ONLY** VENTURE CAPITAL CONGLOMERATE THAT DISRUPTS EVERY BUSINESS IT ENTERS.

TWITTER IS THE **ONLY** SOCIAL MEDIA SERVICE BASED ON 140-CHARACTER MESSAGES.

CIRQUE DU SOLEIL IS THE **ONLY** CIRCUS WITH BROADWAY SOPHISTICATION.

AERON IS THE **ONLY** OFFICE CHAIR THAT REDEFINES ERGONOMIC DESIGN.

TOMS IS THE **ONLY** SHOE COMPANY THAT DONATES ONE PAIR OF SHOES FOR EVERY PAIR IT SELLS.

DISNEY IS THE **ONLY** ENTERTAINMENT COMPANY DEDICATED TO MAGICAL FAMILY EXPERIENCES.

ONLYNESS IS THE SECRET OF POSITIONING

Let's try them out one by one.

"The world's first and only chocolate tea." This isn't true, so it's a non-starter.

"The only tea made from organic cacao husks." Probably not true, and not very compelling.

"The only tea that derives from the Mayans." Interesting, but also not compelling.

"The only tea that is kind to the environment." Even if this were true, there are more effective ways to save the planet.

"The only tea that the whole family will love." Hmm. This could work, given the aims, jobs, and goals of the mom-blogger tribe. The trick is to surround the product with secondary uses and meanings that create barriers to competition. For now, Lori can add it to her Brand Commitment Matrix.

Caution: When staking out your onlyness, remember that whatever seems unique to you may not seem unique to everyone else. YOU'RE viewing your product close up, while THEY'RE seeing it from farther away. Make sure your product is not just unique, but REALLY unique. Crank up the onlyness to eleven. Make it incredibly easy for customers to notice it, choose it, and share it with friends. Don't compete. Differentiate.

PROCESSES ↝ VALUES

The Industrial Age brought with it an emphasis on process. A factory owner could design a process for manufacturing a product, then plug semi-skilled workers into it like parts into a machine. Each worker, each part, would have a limited function, thereby reducing errors and maximizing throughput. This worked amazingly well in a marketplace that was stable and predictable, where power belonged to the manufacturer.

But what would happen if the marketplace were constantly changing? And what if power were in the hands of customers? Would process still be paramount?

The changes came slowly at first. Vending machines began to offer self-service. Catalogs offered products by mail. Service stations asked drivers to pump their own gas. Brokerage firms let people manage their own portfolios. Airlines asked flyers to check themselves in. Publishing companies allowed authors sell their own books. Coming full circle, manufacturers are now helping customers make their own products. The marketplace has flipped.

In today's age of customer control, company processes are still important. But they're subject to increasing flux. They need to be invented and reinvented on the fly, according to the desires and dictates of customers. They can't be developed at the top of the organization and handed down for workers to implement. They must be designed by the workers themselves, often in the moment.

To accomplish this, a company must develop a culture of creative autonomy, guided by a shared understanding of "how we work together" or "how we behave." Company culture is the complement to customer mores, the rules that determine how customers belong to tribes.

The best way to shape company culture is to encourage adherence to a set of values. For example, the world-class experience that Ritz-Carlton provides its guests comes directly from its master value of "service." This value is broken down into 12 sub-values that employees must agree to uphold.

Johnson & Johnson lives by a credo of five responsibilities—to customers, employees, management, communities, and stockholders.

RITZ-CARLTON SERVICE VALUES

1. I build strong relationships and create Ritz-Carlton guests for life.

2. I am always responsive to the expressed and unexpressed wishes and needs of our guests.

3. I am empowered to create unique, memorable, and personal experiences for our guests.

4. I understand my role in achieving the Key Success Factors, embracing Community Footprints and creating the Ritz-Carlton Mystique.

5. I continuously seek opportunities to innovate and improve the Ritz-Carlton experience.

6. I own and immediately resolve guest problems.

7. I create a work environment of teamwork and lateral service so that the needs of our guests and each other are met.

8. I have the opportunity to continuously learn and grow.

9. I am involved in the planning of the work that affects me.

10. I am proud of my professional appearance, language, and behavior.

11. I protect the privacy and security of our guests, my fellow employees, and the company's confidential information and assets.

12. I am responsible for uncompromising levels of cleanliness, and creating a safe and accident-free environment.

This credo has been serving the company well since 1943.

Soap company Method has its "Methodology," five values that express its obsession with culture: 1) keep Method weird, 2) what would MacGyver do? 3) innovate, don't imitate, 4) collaborate, collaborate, collaborate, and 5) care like crazy. These aren't just notions enshrined on the cafeteria wall but living behaviors that are consistently discussed, supported, and rewarded. Founders Eric Ryan and Adam Lowry have discovered that culture provides nearly endless benefits, from boosting employee satisfaction to fostering a cohesive brand and a spirit of innovation. It attracts and keeps better talent, inspires more customers, and helps a company outlast its competitors.

When a company culture goes bad, the brand suffers immediately—eroding revenues, tribal trust, and customer loyalty. For example, the flurry of vehicle recalls by Toyota in 2010 was the direct result of a breakdown in company culture. A former executive, Jim Press, blamed the problems on a group of "financially oriented pirates" who, unlike the founding family, "didn't have the character to maintain a customer-first focus."

Lori, as the founder of her company, has an opportunity to set strong standards from day one. Her customer tribe is educated, family-oriented, tech-savvy, food-conscious, community-minded, and eco-concerned. In completing the Brand Commitment Matrix, she understands that cultural values must sync up with customer mores. In other words, "how we behave" must align with "how they belong." Therefore, she decides, the values of her employees should map closely to those of her customers.

Now that she's completed the matrix, what's next? It's time to start building out the brand. Using the matrix, she'll imagine the experiences that will help her customers create their identities.

who they are

why we exist

what they want

what we offer

how they belong

how we behave

CUSTOMERS | COMPANY

IDENTITY ⟷ PURPOSE

BUSY MOTHERS FOCUSED ON SERVING
NUTRITIOUS FOOD, EDUCATING THEIR
KIDS, CREATING GOOD FAMILY MEMORIES,
BUILDING STRONG SOCIAL TIES,
PROTECTING THE ENVIRONMENT, AND
CONTRIBUTING TO THE COMMUNITY

TO CREATE RITUALS THAT
BRING JOY AND HEALTH TO
FAMILIES EVERYWHERE

AIMS ⟷ ONLYNESS

- DELICIOUS EVERYDAY RITUAL
- CAFFEINE-FREE SUBSTITUTE FOR COFFEE
- NO-CAL SUBSTITUTE FOR SUGAR DRINKS
- AFTER-SCHOOL AND AFTER-DINNER TREAT
- ALCOHOL-FREE SOCIAL LUBRICANT
- POLITICAL STATEMENT FOR ENVIRONMENT
- EFFECTIVE FUNDRAISING PRODUCT
- PLATFORM FOR INFORMATION SHARING
- SYMBOL OF CARING PARENTHOOD

THE **ONLY** TEA THAT THE
WHOLE FAMILY WILL LOVE.

MORES ⟷ VALUES

- ARE TRIBAL BUT SELF-ASSURED
- OFTEN DISAGREE WITH MAJORITY VIEWS
- HAVE STRONG OPINIONS ON PARENTING
- BELIEVE IN THE POWER OF FAMILY
- WANT THEIR KIDS TO BE SELF-SUFFICIENT
- ARE OUTSPOKEN AND ARTICULATE
- AVOID FAST-FOOD RESTAURANTS
- TEND TO SHOP ONLINE
- CARE ABOUT THE SOURCE OF PRODUCTS
- ARE ACTIVE IN THEIR KIDS' SCHOOLING
- JOIN COMMUNITY ACTIVITIES

FAMILY-ORIENTED
FOOD-CONSCIOUS
TECH-SAVVY
COMMUNITY-MINDED
ECO-AWARE

The best brands are vivid. They conjure clear mental pictures and powerful feelings in the minds and hearts of customers. They come to life through their TOUCHPOINTS, the points at which customers experience them—from the first exposure to a brand's name, to buying the product, to using it and eventually making it part of who they are.

Here's how the Ritz looks at touchpoints, as written in the company's credo: "The Ritz-Carlton experience enlivens the senses, instills well-being, and fulfills even the unexpressed wishes and needs of our guests."

If the Ritz were to focus on features instead of experience, their credo might read: "We offer clean, expensively appointed rooms, scented soaps and towels, and a well-trained staff." This second version is true, but not inspiring. It's a lifeless list of features instead of a living contract between committed employees and their guests. Judging only by these two statements, which hotel would you choose?

Let's break the credo into its three components:

"Enlivens the senses." This phrase talks about the aesthetics of the hotel—the quality of its architecture, interior design, furnishings, art, fabrics, textures, aromas, sounds, tastes, and the relationships among them.

"Instills well-being." Well-being is hard to define, but we all know it when we feel it. It's the welcome experience of comfort, calm, and control over our day. The Ritz imparts this through its warm staff, orderly processes, and unobtrusive efficiency.

"Fulfills even the unexpressed wishes and needs of our guests." Here the Ritz sets the bar high. Expressed needs are one thing. But unexpressed wishes? There are only two ways to achieve this: the analysis of many data points over time, and the practical application of empathy. The Ritz clearly knows its customers well enough to anticipate their wishes. But the same can be said of companies such as Amazon, Apple, Method, Nordstrom, and Zappos, who use some combination of analysis and empathy to better serve their customers.

Together, empathy and analysis can create a virtuous circle of improvement. Take customer call centers. Most companies see customer service as a cost to be minimized, relegating it to lower-level employees or external vendors. This is shortsighted—there's no other way to say it. A customer call is the moment of truth for a brand. It's a brief time of heightened experience for a customer, one that can either drive her away or cement a lifelong relationship. The best move for many large companies, some have suggested, would be to send that excess executive pay to the front lines where it can do some real good.

The founders of Method agree that it's counterproductive to outsource customer calls to India. "The customer has actually used your product. This isn't just a marketing opportunity; it's a chance to capture new insights, create a raving fan, and even safeguard yourself from legal problems." Customer calls can be turned into what the Academy of Marketing Science calls "transcendent customer experiences"—emotional encounters that generate lasting shifts in beliefs and attitudes, and sometimes even self-transformation.

Think of brand experiences as "fractals" of the overall brand. Each experience is the brand in miniature, a representative sample of what your customers understand about the company and its offerings. If you find that a particular experience doesn't reflect your overall brand, pull it out. It's a weed in an otherwise purposeful garden. Every experience, every touchpoint, should illustrate the meaning of the brand and offer another way for your customers to build their identities.

In practice, which touchpoints work best, and how many should you have? The short answers are 1) the most telling touchpoints, and 2) as few as possible. The more touchpoints you create, the more complexity and cost you introduce into the business. At the same time, you want to give customers as much access to your brand as possible, anytime and anywhere. Let me suggest a two-step process for developing your touchpoints.

First, draw up a list of all the touchpoints that make sense for your brand. You can choose from the menu on the following page, then add others that are particular to your brand. Next, grade each touchpoint from one to five points, one being for the least-aligned or cost-effective opportunities, and five being for the opportunities that might produce transcendent customer experiences that your brand can own and defend.

Arrange your touchpoints on the Brand Experience Map on page 75. Notice that the map

SHALLOW

COMPANY BLOG
NEWSLETTERS
WORD OF MOUTH
SOCIAL MEDIA
CUSTOMER RATINGS
WEBSITE NAVIGATION
STORE DESIGN
ARCHITECTURE
POINT OF SALE
MOBILE APPS
MARKETING EMAILS
FOLLOW-UPS
THANK-YOU CARDS
LOYALTY PROGRAM
PERSONAL OFFERS
UNBOXING EXPERIENCE
SERVICE ADVISORS
MONTHLY STATEMENTS
ACCOUNT ALERTS
APPLICATION FORMS
SALES PITCHES
PRODUCT DEMOS
TRADESHOW BOOTH

NAME
TRADEMARK
TAGLINE
ELEVATOR PITCH
PRODUCT DESIGN
CATALOG
WEBSITE CONTENT
BROCHURE
BUSINESS CARDS
PACKAGING
PRICING
MEDIA ARTICLES
PRODUCT PLACEMENT
ADVERTISING
SIGNAGE
VEHICLE GRAPHICS

GENERAL ← → PERSONAL

FOUNDING STORY
THOUGHT LEADERSHIP
BOOK PUBLISHING
PARTNERSHIPS
EMPLOYEE BEHAVIORS
WELCOME PACKET
KEYNOTE SPEECHES
COMMUNITY GIVEBACKS
SPONSORSHIPS

FREE SAMPLES
PRODUCT USE
USER'S MANUAL
CUSTOMER REVIEWS
BRAND ADVOCACY
INTRA-TRIBE DISCUSSION
PERSONAL BUSINESS
SEMINARS
WORKSHOPS
IN-STORE CLASSES
CUSTOMER EVENTS
OPEN HOUSES
CALL CENTER

DEEP

TOUCHPOINT MENU

has two axes, one that runs from the general to the personal, and one that runs from shallow to deep. Populate the map with touchpoints in each quadrant, so that customers will be able to encounter a range of experiences on their journey from awareness to commitment.

Lori, of course, needs to launch her brand with the least number of touchpoints, both to control costs and to keep her brand simple while she's learning about it. Naturally, she'll need the basics— a name, logo, package, and website, and the messaging that will establish her product's difference. These touchpoints will fall in the SHALLOW/GENERAL quadrant, where brand awareness begins.

She'll also need some experiences in the DEEP/ GENERAL quadrant, where the touchpoints are more tribal. These might include the product's backstory, thought leadership, keynote addresses, and offers of free samples. Later she might expand into chocolate tea cookbooks, sponsorships, and community givebacks. She may eventually write a how-I-did-it book like Howard Schultz did with POUR YOUR HEART INTO IT, about the rise of Starbucks.

In the SHALLOW/PERSONAL quadrant, she could include social media such as Twitter, Facebook,

Instagram, and Pinterest. She could design the shipping boxes and the "unboxing" experience to address her customers' interests in elegant objects and environmental responsibility. She could make her website as easy to use and addictive as her chocolate tea. She could send informative email blasts, write blog articles, and issue hand-signed thank-you cards to first-time customers.

Finally, in the DEEP/PERSONAL quadrant, she could begin to turn over control to her customers. This is where they can use her product to build their identities, expand the tribe, and turn the brand into a mini-movement. She could run workshops, classes, and community events. She could develop a special corps of "chocolateers," alpha-customers who host tea parties or write guest articles for the website.

And where to sell the product? It's always best to keep it small and simple to start with. She can begin to sell it from her website, and later expand to stores, such as Whole Foods, as the company builds momentum. Later, if she allows herself to dream big, she might consider opening kiosks in shopping centers, or even a national chain of tea shops.

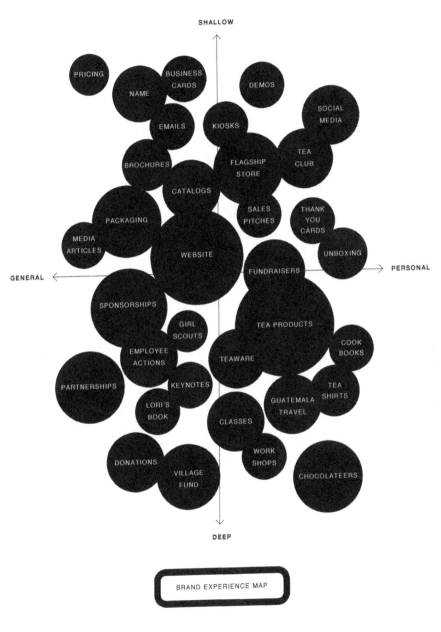

SHALLOW

PRICING
BUSINESS CARDS
NAME
DEMOS
SOCIAL MEDIA
EMAILS
KIOSKS
TEA CLUB
BROCHURES
FLAGSHIP STORE
CATALOGS
SALES PITCHES
THANK YOU CARDS
PACKAGING
MEDIA ARTICLES
WEBSITE
UNBOXING

GENERAL ← → PERSONAL

FUNDRAISERS
SPONSORSHIPS
GIRL SCOUTS
TEA PRODUCTS
EMPLOYEE ACTIONS
TEAWARE
COOK BOOKS
PARTNERSHIPS
KEYNOTES
TEA SHIRTS
LORI'S BOOK
GUATEMALA TRAVEL
CLASSES
DONATIONS
VILLAGE FUND
WORK SHOPS
CHOCOLATEERS

DEEP

BRAND EXPERIENCE MAP

You might think customer experience is all work and no profit. But you'd be wrong. Research has shown that experience is one of the richest areas to mine for shareholder value. Watermark Consulting analyzed the stock performance of the leaders in customer experience, as measured by Forrester Research's Customer Experience Index. Returns over a six-year period were up 43 percent for customer-experience leaders and down 33.9 percent for customer-experience laggards. Another study showed that experience leaders outstripped the S&P 500 by a full 26 percent. Yet, as Forrester analysts said, "marketing remains stuck in messaging mode."

By the time you read this chapter, discount airline Ryanair will be doing one of two things: 1) improving its treatment of customers, or 2) losing market share to more enlightened competitors.

In a 2015 survey, brand firm Siegel+Gale named Ryanair the world's second worst brand after insurance company AXA. This is actually an improvement over other studies, which put the company at the very bottom.

"If we're the worst-performing brand in the world," said Ryanair CEO Michael O'Leary, "why are we the biggest international airline in the world?" Short answer: The biggest company and the best brand are two different things. Time will tell. A bad brand is usually a leading indicator of a company headed for trouble.

Let's say you want to book a flight from London to Rome. You go to the Ryanair website and choose a round-trip flight. Pretty cheap, even with the modest credit card fee. You click "continue." You add baggage fees of $140. The seats on Ryanair don't recline. There's not enough legroom to be comfortable, so you reserve a seat with slightly more space for $15. You see that you're now up to twice the original investment. What you don't see is that, if your bags are overweight when you get to the airport, you'll pay an additional $11 per pound on the spot. And if you've forgotten to print your boarding pass at home, you'll owe another $100 in penalties.

These are only the financial costs. When you board the plane, exhausted from your ordeal at the airport, peace and quiet are not to be yours. The PA system blares "special deals" for much of the flight. You arrive in Rome with a pounding headache, wishing you had booked on any other airline. You now realize that the costs of flying Ryanair are much higher than they seemed.

Ryanair may be an example of a punitive brand, but it's not the only one. Insurance companies like AXA are famous for failing to protect customers against the very calamities they buy policies for.

Blockbuster Video used to charge so much in late fees that its customers eventually defected to the more fair-minded Netflix.

Wireless carriers typically use contracts instead of loyalty to lock people in. This allowed lock-in-free T-Mobile to steal millions of their competitors' unhappy customers. And on the discount airline front, Southwest has won the hearts and minds

WHAT GOES UP
MUST COME DOWN
FOR COMPANIES
THAT PUNISH THEIR
CUSTOMERS WITH
BAD EXPERIENCES.

of flyers by announcing its "Bags Fly Free" policy to contrast with the fee-grabbing moves of competitors.

A recent study discovered an 80/80 rule: 80 percent of business is service, and 80 percent of customers report bad service. Companies that punish their customers are fair game for flipped brands. Netflix, T-Mobile, Southwest, and others have taken full advantage of the 80/80 rule—by breaking it.

Marketing psychologist Kit Yarrow notes that customers want five things from a purchasing decision: 1) to feel more in control, 2) to reduce the fear of making a mistake, 3) to simplify the decision process, 4) to offer clear and immediate emotional benefits, and 5) to be free of obstacles. Of these five, she says, customer control is the best "antidote to anxiety." Anxiety goes far to explain the extraordinary power of customer reviews.

Psychology professor Ryan Martin says that although we tend to share the happiness of people we are closest to, we are quite willing to join the "rage of strangers" when we're unhappy. Rage claims immediate attention on social media. A full 80 percent of purchasers say they've changed their minds after reading a single negative review.

How can you avoid the wrath of customers who feel wronged? By flipping your brand from customer punishment to customer protection.

Start by uncovering the hidden costs, risks, irritations, anxieties, and points of confusion in your customer interactions. What keeps them from buying? Why do they exit your website mid-purchase? What are their questions when they call customer service? How can you reduce their anxiety? Eliminate boredom? Make customers feel central and give them control?

One tool you can apply is FORGIVENESS. Forgiveness is a concept that took root in user-interface design. It includes features like "Undo," for when you change your mind; "Did you mean..." for when you've made a mistake: "Are you sure..." before you make an important decision, "Auto save" to keep you from starting over, and the ability to come back to your last screen after you exit. A forgiving format is one that accepts various kinds of user input and lets the system sort it out.

Netflix CEO Reed Hastings employs forgiveness to create "subscriber happiness." He makes sure it's ultra-simple for customers to quit the service any time without a penalty. If the exit door is well marked, he reasons, subscribers will be more likely to come back.

Progressive, unlike other car insurance companies, protects its customers at the moment of highest anxiety: the accident. An adjuster drives to the scene, calms the claimant's fears, and calls for a replacement car. In most cases he settles the claim then and there and hands the customer a check.

WHAT CAN YOU FIX?

Is the product hard to find or buy?

Are there unseen costs that customers must incur?

What are the hidden risks or obstacles?

Are there features that cause anxiety or confusion?

Can you deliver the product or service better?

Can you save the customer some time?

Does your store or business have easy parking?

Is checkout fast and friendly?

Can you make the product easier to understand?

Is your instruction manual too long or hard to follow?

Can you make customers feel better?

Is the product or packaging easy to recycle?

Are there opportunities to produce savings?

Can you eliminate negative social consequences?

Is it possible to offer 24-hour service?

What can Lori do to show kindness and empathy toward her customers? First, she can make her offerings very clear by describing the products, the tea-making process, the number of servings per box, and the demonstrable benefits of using the product. Second, she can design her website to make navigation truly intuitive by anticipating the desires and questions of her customers —the "unexpressed wishes and needs" that Ritz-Carlton cares so much about. Third, she can amortize basic shipping costs into the price to remove the "stinger" at the end of the transaction. Finally, she can make it easy for customers to review the product, ask questions, and make unedited comments right on the site.

Polls for Y&R'S Brand Asset Valuator indicate that customers' expectations for "kindness and empathy" have increased 391 percent in recent years. Companies ignore this shift at their peril. As Kit Yarrow says, "Once it was CAVEAT EMPTOR [buyer beware], but now it's more like CAVEAT VENDITOR [seller beware]. Hell hath no fury like a scorned shopper." While many companies are addressing this, some are offering more kindness and empathy than others. The difference is design.

PART 3 : DESIGNING THE WAY FORWARD

DECIDING ↗ DESIGNING

You can't DECIDE a great customer experience.
You have to DESIGN it. Designing is the only way
to create a vibrant set of touchpoints that enable
customers to fully engage with your brand. Unfortunately, most of us were trained for the DECIDING
mode. We were taught to memorize, analyze,
debate, and defend. These are valuable skills, but
to excel at creative tasks we also need to imagine,
intuit, visualize, and prototype. The designing
mode is what flips branding from mere mimicry
to strategic differentiation.

Let me say right from the top that brand experience is the province of pros. Very few great touchpoints have been designed by amateurs—or by
accident. To become a designer requires a level of
inborn talent, a multiyear investment in education
and internship, and 5–10 years of focused practice
to develop a dependable set of skills. Even within
the design community, professionals agree that only
about 5 percent of designers are exceptional.

Where does that leave you? If you're a designer,
you're probably straining and stretching every day
to reach the top 5 percent. If you're a manager,
you'll need to find the most proficient designers

you can and learn how to tease out their best work. This is precisely what Steve Jobs did at Apple. He took young designers from school and put them in a school-like setting—a culture that not only supported, but insisted on, great design.

Design is difficult to explain, but it's easy to demonstrate. It reveals itself more easily through artifacts than language. The process starts by imagining or reimagining a wide variety of solutions—some bad, some wrong, and many only so-so. Out of this session may come a few good ideas, which can then be mocked up, amped up, and refined to reach their potential.

Luckily, Lori had some practice working with creative professionals in her last two jobs. She decides to host a "creative swarm," an intense, workshop-like session with a cross-functional team. She assembles a small group of freelancers—a graphic designer, web designer, copywriter, product designer, and researcher—to prototype the major touchpoints for her brand over a one-week period.

On day one, she and the group focus on the SHALLOW/GENERAL quadrant of the Brand Experience Map. This is where the basic brand elements reside, such as the name, trademark, packaging, and website. There are no boundaries placed on the work. If an idea for a tagline leads to an idea for a customer event, both are fair game. The goal is to imagine as many ideas as possible.

By the end of the first morning the team has Okoko, Tekoko, Rokoko, and Koko Maya. These all contain the word fragment "koko," suggesting the ideas of "cocoa" and "cacao." They also have a Mayan or jungle flavor, which might lead to some distinctive brand expressions. Moreover, these words pass the seven tests of a good brand name: distinctiveness (does it stands out?), brevity (does it have four syllables or fewer?), appropriateness (does it fit the brand?), easy pronunciation (is it easy to say?), likability (do you WANT to say it?), and extendability (does it lends itself to brand play?), and protectability (can we trademark it?).

The designers take the names and start sketching logos and packaging ideas. After an hour or so, Lori shares an insight: What if the brand adopted a character to symbolize it? Maybe a Mayan animal like a bird, a frog, or a dragon. "Or a monkey," adds the researcher. A monkey! Monkeys are social, curious, creative, mischievous, and smart.

The team decides to try it.

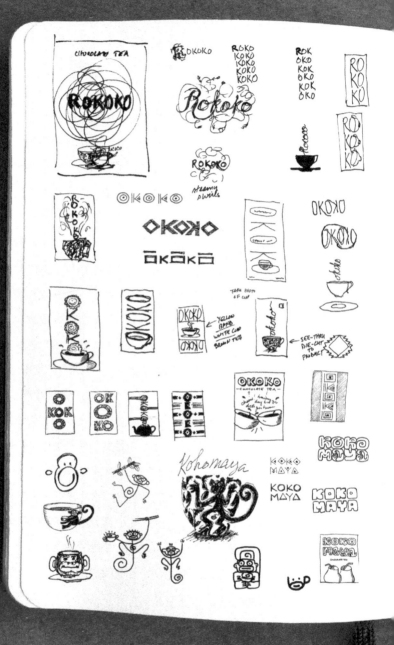

From name to character to logo to package to website, they skip across various touchpoints, checking back with each other for occasional validation, feedback, or inspiration. In the process of exploration, ideas for other touchpoints arise—teaware, an online video, a cookbook, an educational fund for Guatemalan children. After three days they have an impressive number of ideas to place on the Brand Experience Map.

The object of the map is to make sure each of the four quadrants contains enough great touchpoints so that customers can find their way from a passing interest in the brand to a rich engagement with it. Of course, not all customers will engage deeply, nor can all brands offer the kind of depth that will create a lifelong commitment. For example, I love peanut M&Ms, but I haven't based my identity on them (so far).

The best quadrant for fostering commitment is the DEEP/PERSONAL one. Here's where you begin to hand control of the brand to customers. You help them find special jobs in the context of the tribe—jobs that let them express their personalities, add social capital to their lives, help them build their skills, make a difference, or even make money.

Lori's team comes up with ideas for social interaction, such as a tea-party catering service, school fundraisers with tea sales, and classes and workshops for cooking with chocolate tea. To be compelling, each of these ideas will need to be DESIGNED, *not just* DECIDED.

Does design pay off?

The Design Management Institute partnered with Motiv Strategies to measure the return on design investment where it counts—in stock values. Over a 10-year period, a $10,000 investment in design-centric companies would have yielded returns 228 percent greater than the same investment in the S&P 500. And this is only an average.

Companies that approach design with more rigor can do even better. Car manufacturer Mini found that "design" is the reason 80 percent of its customers give for buying its cars. Yet it spends only one percent of its total budget on it. The success of design is not determined by how much you spend, but how you spend it.

PLANS ⌀ EXPERIMENTS

There's an old adage in business: If you fail to plan, you plan to fail. Yet plans fail all the time. You research the market, crunch the numbers, build a budget, outline the steps, and place them on a timeline. Nice and tidy. And then your plan meets reality in a head-on collision. The market ignores your product, sales don't hit targets, costs run over, and everything takes longer than it should. Your business dies a quick death and investors lose their shirts.

Why does this happen? Because plans—specifically those involving innovation—are necessarily based on faulty assumptions. There's no way to predict whether or not the market will embrace a new product, service, feature, or business model. There are too many unknowns. To succeed in a dynamic market, you have to flip your approach from planning to experimenting.

In his book THE INNOVATOR'S HYPOTHESIS, Michael Schrage says that plans are based on a presumption of knowledge, whereas experiments are based on a presumption of ignorance. It's better to learn offstage so you can triumph onstage. "Innovation amateurs talk good ideas," he says.

"Innovation experts talk testable hypotheses,"

A hypothesis, embodied as a prototype, beats market research because it can be tested. The word PROTOTYPE comes from the Greek words PROTOS and TYPOS, meaning "first form." Customers don't have to imagine how they would feel when they see a prototype. They're already feeling it. Steve Jobs, although famous for rejecting market research, insisted that Apple designers make and test hundreds of prototypes before deciding on the final form of a new product.

The secret to great prototypes is to design them quickly and cheaply. Music producer Nick Lowe earned the nickname Basher for telling his recording artists to "bash it out now and tart it up later." You can't arrange a song theoretically. You have to try out various elements and make improvements as you go. Same with a product or a business model. The quicker and cheaper the better.

Designing is thinking with your hands. Start with a scribble. See what's missing, what could be improved, what else it reminds you of. Make more scribbles. Work the best scribbles into low-fidelity prototypes—limited function mockups, models, or experiences that you can test in the real world.

The goal isn't to impress your customers, but to let them impress you with their reactions, knowledge, and insights. Think of design as a rich conversation that brings you closer to the truth of your brand.

Lori and her team have already produced a number of prototypes that are ready to test. These include versions of the name, logo, package, and website. Testing will not only help narrow the field to the most promising, but will suggest small improvements that could make a big difference to the overall customer experience.

She and her researcher set up Skype calls with 25 potential customers to gather feedback on names, logos, packages, and website options. To Lori's surprise, the participants favor Koko Maya over the other names, finding it more fun to pronounce and more descriptive of the product. Their reactions to the packages reinforce their preference for the name. The prototype with the monkey is a clear winner with respondents, especially if a few modest changes could be made.

Armed with new information, Lori goes back to the design team to refocus the work. Now they can home in on one direction and reduce the number of touchpoints to those with the greatest "wow."

PEOPLE DIDN'T
CONNECT THE
"T" WITH "TEA,"
AND COULDN'T
MAKE OUT THE
MEANING OF
THE PACKAGE

PEOPLE NOTED
THE LACK OF
A "JUNGLE" THEME,
ALTHOUGH THEY
APPRECIATED
THE PACKAGE'S
SIMPLE CHARM

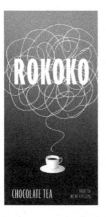

RESPONDENTS
LOVED THE NAME
AND THE MONKEY,
BUT FOUND THE
GRAPHICS TOO
CHILDLIKE

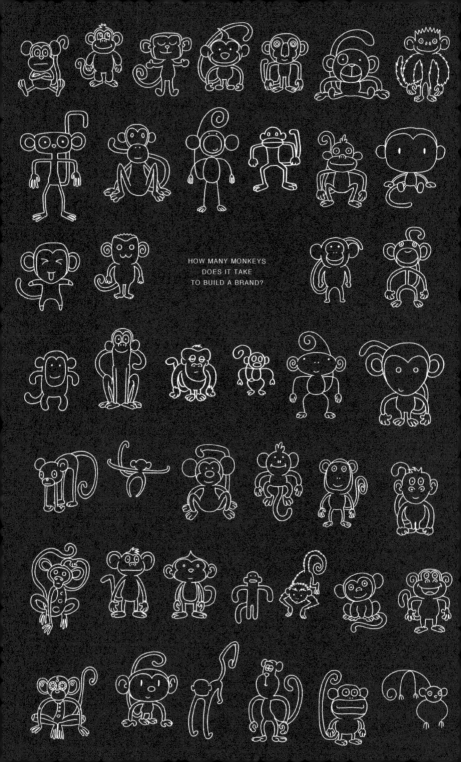

HOW MANY MONKEYS
DOES IT TAKE
TO BUILD A BRAND?

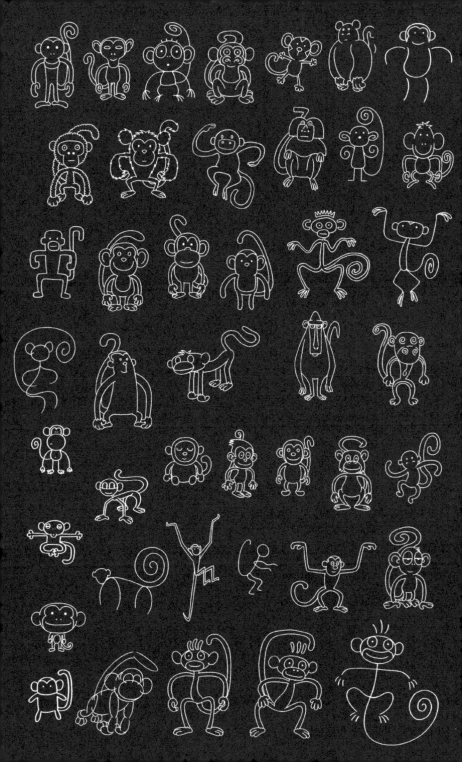

CUSTOMERS
WERE INTRIGUED
BY THE MAYAN
MONKEY KING,
BUT WERE LESS
IMPRESSED WITH
THE OVERALL
PACKAGE

WHILE PEOPLE
WERE DRAWN TO
THE CUTE MONKEY,
THEY FELT THAT
THE PACKAGE
IN GENERAL
WAS BORING

THIS PACKAGE
WAS POPULAR,
BUT MOST PEOPLE
HAD DIFFICULTY
CONNECTING
IT WITH TEA

CUSTOMERS
LOVED THIS
STRETCHING
MONKEY,
BUT FOUND IT
HARD TO READ
THE NAME

OVERCHOICE ↻ SIMPLICITY

The first thing companies did with computer technology back in the 1980s was to multiply the number of choices for their customers. More colors, more styles, more features, more models, more messages, more channels, more services, more brand extensions, more SKUs. The siren call of "consumer choice" proved impossible for companies to resist. If a little choice was good, they reasoned, more choice was better.

Customers loved it. For about 15 minutes. Today their lives are so cluttered by choice that they can barely breathe. Americans now see that a little choice increases their freedom, but too much takes it away. Do you really want to spend three hours learning how to use the features on your new Samsung TV? Or sort through 17 varieties each time you buy Crest toothpaste at the supermarket? Or deal with the 3,000 pages of items shown in Restoration Hardware's 15-pound set of catalogs? Not if you have a life.

Of course, none of us wants to give up this lavish banquet of choice. We just want it off the floor and out of the way. "It's not information overload," media consultant Clay Shirky famously said. "It's filter failure." Our brains can't handle the deluge. We're desperate for a way to organize, access, and make use of so many options. Amazon founder Jeff Bezos called it "cognitive overhead."

For flipped companies, the deluge of over-choice is an opportunity. The same technology that created customer choice can be used to simplify it. This is what Larry Page and Sergey Brin saw in 1998 when they launched Google. Their refresh-ingly simple home page was a life raft in an ocean of data, promising users a simple benefit—the ability to find something fast. Other smart com-panies are now following suit. They're using design to remove clutter and give people back their lives.

Why do companies create clutter in the first place? Why not start simple, like Google did, and just keep it simple? Because simplicity has many enemies. It takes great clarity, courage, and discipline to vanquish them.

The list on the following page contains the top seven enemies of simplicity, starting with the most common: the human impulse to add. Whenever I ask workshop participants to come up with ideas to improve a brand, they'll rarely grab for the sub-traction tool. Instead they'll invent more features,

THE SEVEN ENEMIES OF SIMPLICITY

1. **THE URGE TO ADD.** Most of us have a strong tendency toward creating "more," even when less would be better.

2. **THE DESIRE TO MAKE A MARK.** Another strong tendency is the desire for "brand children"—features, products, services, and businesses that we can name and point to with pride.

3. **THE NEED TO GROW REVENUES.** Selling more stuff leads to higher profits, doesn't it? It's a common perception, but not always true.

4. **THE LURE OF COMPETITON.** Marketers often find it easier to play an existing game than to change the rules or start a different game, so they focus on one-upmanship instead.

5. **THE FEAR OF FALLING BEHIND.** If one company adds a hot new feature, panic sets in. Fast-following companies will feel the need to match that feature, usually without subtracting others.

6. **THE EXPEDIENCY OF EXTENSION.** Brand extensions, the process of adding variations to an existing product or service, often produce profits in the short term (at the risk of defocusing the brand).

7. **THE MASKING OF WEAK DESIGN.** It's easier to obscure a poor design with more details than to make the fewest number of details count. Designers refer to these cover-ups as "band-aids."

services, versions, or variations. This seems to be a deeply human tendency.

Constant addition without subtraction always makes a mess. One cluttered home page is indistinguishable from another cluttered home page. One "comprehensive" service looks a lot like another comprehensive service. One convoluted business is no different—nor better—than another one. A mess is counterproductive when you're trying to create meaningful differentiation for your brand.

A better approach is to flip your thinking. Keep vigilance against creeping messiness. Delight in the minimal, the ultra clear, the super simple. Never add without trying to subtract. Take courage in what G. K. Chesterton said: "The simplification of anything is always sensational."

Lori and her team are awash in prototypes. They have too many ideas for one startup to manage, and more than enough to delight customers in the short term. Lori decides to focus on the few that will make the most difference, and put the rest on the back burner. For the launch, she'll go with the name, the logo, one product, the packaging, the website, and social media. She'll watch what works and what doesn't, and build out from there.

STATIC BRANDS ↻ LIQUID BRANDS

We live in a time of "meta change," a period in which the very nature of change is changing. It's speeding up to the point where competitive advantage is measured in months instead of years. And the direction of change has become much more turbulent. Information flows not only from top to bottom, but from bottom to top, side to side, and a hundred other ways all at once.

It's no longer possible for a business to build a monolithic brand on top of a built-to-last strategy. Instead, it has to flip into a new mode, one that can adapt to change, enroll customers on their own terms, and relinquish more control of the brand to advocates.

Flipping the brand triggers a "phase change"—a structural shift from a company-focused business to a customer-focused business. Think of a solid changing into a liquid, or ice melting into water. Now it has the ability to flow, to find new ways forward, to adapt to changing circumstances, and to touch everyone and everything in its path. A flipped brand can course forward across platforms, through channels, over boundaries, and into touchpoints. It can branch out to adjacent markets and braid itself into larger revenue streams.

Martin Weigel, a planner at advertising agency Wieden+Kennedy, thinks brands are becoming more like software. "Brands can now remember what we like, and what we bought," he says. "They can anticipate when we need to restock, repurchase, or renew. They can suggest purchases, content, and experiences we will probably like. They can compare and recommend purchase options. They can respond to our service, upgrade, and replacement needs." As brands become unshackled from the constraints of bricks and mortar, he suggests, they become more fluid.

This is the future that Liquid Agency (my own company) envisioned when it opened its doors over a decade ago. As CEO Scott Gardner said, "Today's companies need brands that can touch people wherever they are. Brands need to be adaptive so they can flow like liquid through our lives."

What this means for managers is a new way of building brands. Instead of a once-and-done exercise, branding is a continuing story told by both the company and its customers. It's not a checklist but an endless storyboard. While well-defined plans are still necessary, they need to be rolling plans, subject to change as the game unfolds. A strategy meeting should not be an annual summit but a monthly exercise in course correction. Plan the work, then work the plan.

Brands can no longer afford to be static. They need to grow, spread, and flow into new areas. This is known as BRANCHING, the art of sequencing markets. For example, BMW is branching from gas and diesel cars to "urban mobility" cars with its BMWi electric vehicle. From there it can move into premium mobility services, including apps for traffic, parking, and other real-time information. Next, it can form a venture group to finance startups, and eventually create co-brands with them. These are new revenue streams that spring from the company's original vision of high-performance transportation vehicles.

Every brand is a running narrative, a story-in-progress whose hero is the customer. If at any point the story splits into two stories aimed at two different tribes, you then have two brands. To keep the narrative together, each new feature, extension, or product use must keep something from the original direction to preserve logical continuity.

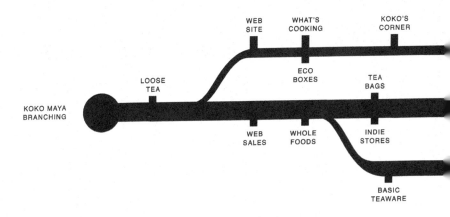

KOKO MAYA
BRANCHING

WEB
SITE

WHAT'S
COOKING

KOKO'S
CORNER

LOOSE
TEA

ECO
BOXES

TEA
BAGS

WEB
SALES

WHOLE
FOODS

INDIE
STORES

BASIC
TEAWARE

YEAR ONE

YEAR TWO

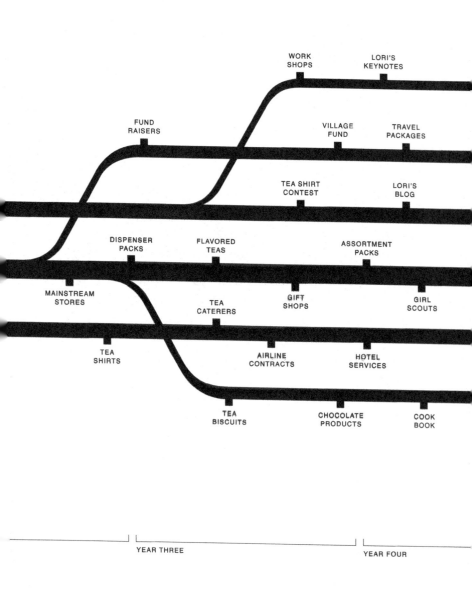

WORK
SHOPS

LORI'S
KEYNOTES

FUND
RAISERS

VILLAGE
FUND

TRAVEL
PACKAGES

TEA SHIRT
CONTEST

LORI'S
BLOG

DISPENSER
PACKS

FLAVORED
TEAS

ASSORTMENT
PACKS

MAINSTREAM
STORES

TEA
CATERERS

GIFT
SHOPS

GIRL
SCOUTS

TEA
SHIRTS

AIRLINE
CONTRACTS

HOTEL
SERVICES

TEA
BISCUITS

CHOCOLATE
PRODUCTS

COOK
BOOK

YEAR THREE

YEAR FOUR

DESIGNING THE WAY FORWARD

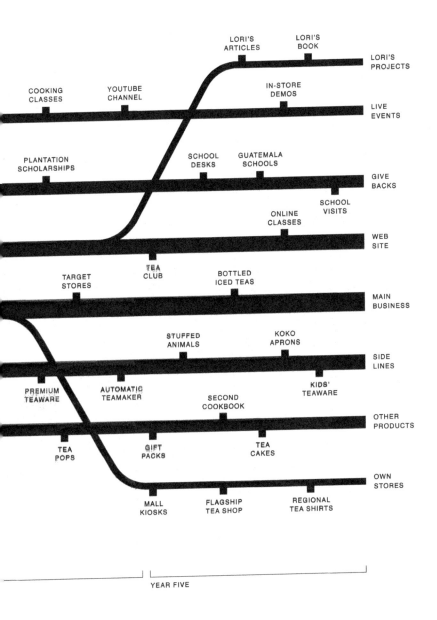

LORI'S
ARTICLES

LORI'S
BOOK

LORI'S
PROJECTS

COOKING
CLASSES

YOUTUBE
CHANNEL

IN-STORE
DEMOS

LIVE
EVENTS

PLANTATION
SCHOLARSHIPS

SCHOOL
DESKS

GUATEMALA
SCHOOLS

GIVE
BACKS

SCHOOL
VISITS

ONLINE
CLASSES

WEB
SITE

TARGET
STORES

TEA
CLUB

BOTTLED
ICED TEAS

MAIN
BUSINESS

STUFFED
ANIMALS

KOKO
APRONS

SIDE
LINES

KIDS'
TEAWARE

PREMIUM
TEAWARE

AUTOMATIC
TEAMAKER

SECOND
COOKBOOK

OTHER
PRODUCTS

TEA
POPS

GIFT
PACKS

TEA
CAKES

OWN
STORES

MALL
KIOSKS

FLAGSHIP
TEA SHOP

REGIONAL
TEA SHIRTS

YEAR FIVE

For example, a successful toothpaste product could branch into a mouthwash product, or the company could market a special electric toothbrush. Either of these would be logical "plot moves" for the brand. But if it suddenly veered off into cosmetics, customers might feel lost. They might easily close the book on the brand.

Lori tries to imagine how Koko Maya's story might unfold. She might start by selling loose tea in a box, pure and simple—an intriguing new product with a stylish presentation. In this scenario, the website would be the only sales channel. During the first year, customer and mom-blogger feedback would lead to improvements in the product, the packaging, the website, and delivery methods. From there the product might move into organic grocery stores like Whole Foods.

At that point, the credibility of being seen at retail could pave the way for a line extension, maybe a tea-bag version of the product. This could be tested online, and if successful, sold into mass-market grocery stores that prefer more convenient products. With two versions and a larger following, Lori could think about introducing side products such as a line of teaware, and perhaps a few "tea shirts" featuring Koko the monkey. She could hold an online competition for new shirts designed by customers and their kids.

Meanwhile, she might invest in the plantation communities where her product is sourced. At first, she might simply make donations to the local schools to use for books and sports equipment. Later, she might set up travel opportunities, so families and schoolchildren could take trips to Guatemala to experience its culture. She could also specify that a certain percentage of Koko Maya's profits be used to help the plantation villages improve their infrastructure—electricity, water, sanitation, and health care.

At this point kokomaya.com would start to become more than an e-commerce site. It would serve as a community gathering place—a town hall where customers and non-customers could find healthy recipes, information about school fundraising opportunities, and news of cocoa-based cooking classes. It would host conversations among engaged customers who want to share information on child rearing, community involvement, and environmental issues.

Koko Maya would begin to take on the complexion of a mini-movement. The tea itself, once merely a product, would become something more—a symbol of a rich family life, a building block in the identity of its customers.

To turn vision into reality, Lori places these milestones and others on a five-year timeline. She checks to see if each step can generate enough profits to support the next, and that each step is modest, logical, and well aligned with the POV side of the Brand Commitment Matrix. Each quarter she'll update the timeline to reflect changes in the company's ongoing narrative.

But what about the IAM side of the matrix? What stories will Lori's customers tell?

As the nature of change changes, so does the nature of stories.

Media theorist Douglas Rushkoff wrote a fascinating book called PRESENT SHOCK, in which he claims we're losing our capacity to absorb traditional narrative. Technology has taken away our interest in "anything that isn't happening right now" and replaced it with "everything that supposedly is."

Once upon a time, stories could hold aud- iences captive. For example, TV commercials could introduce a damsel, place her in distress, and pitch a product that will save her—all in 30 seconds. Today 30 seconds of commercial nar- rative is too long. Viewers are not only bored with one-way conversations, but annoyed that some- one they don't trust would try to steal their time.

We now live in a world of participatory theater in which we watch a performance and simultane- ously judge the performer—not unlike Japanese bunraku, in which we see not only the puppets but the puppeteers. We're no longer content to sit in the audience and follow the story. We want to go backstage, examine the props and

BRANDING IS NOW
LIKE BUNRAKU THEATER,
IN WHICH THE AUDIENCE
JUDGES BOTH THE PUPPETS
AND THE PUPPETEERS.

the rigging, discover the story behind the story.

"What if stories themselves are incompatible with a presentist culture?" asks Rushkoff. "How then do we maintain a sense of purpose and meaning?" He believes that a lack of regard for beginnings and endings—our focus on the per-petual now—is forcing us to create our own order. We build our own stories as a way of "bounding our experience and limiting our sense of limbo." Narrativity is becoming less like a book and more like a jigsaw puzzle that we put together by making connections and recognizing patterns.

For marketers who understand this, the collapse of narrative is not such a bad thing. It's almost impossible for a company to tell a consistent story anyway, since there's no single "writer," and every member of the audience has a different viewing angle. Moreover, customers don't want to be TOLD, they want to TELL. They long to be the heroes of their own journeys. Marketers need to pull back on storytelling and focus on STORYFRAMING.

Storyframing is the discipline of building a structure that lets customers create their own narratives. It provides the boundaries that keep the story contained, like the edges of the jigsaw puzzle. The basic framework includes the POV of the company—its purpose, onlyness, and values, plus the IAM of the customer—personal identity, customer aims, and tribal mores. Out of the framework comes a range of encounters, or touchpoints, through which customers can find personal meaning and growth. The job of the company is to keep the framework alive while encouraging and applauding its customers.

When all the stories of all the customers are woven together, they make one big story. The big story should impart a feeling of "profluence," a word coined by writer John Gardner to describe the forward flow of a narrative—the feeling that the story is "going somewhere." Without profluence, brands lose momentum and customers lose interest. Think of what happened to brands such as Sears, Radio Shack, Kodak, Chrysler, and Blackberry. Their story frames ended up broken, boring, and bankrupt of meaning. There's little there that customers can use for story material.

How will Lori's customers tell their stories? Will they be able to create profluence in their

Once upon a time a little ▮▮▮▮▮ named ▮▮▮▮▮ went for a long walk in the ▮▮▮▮▮ and was suddenly greeted by a ▮▮▮▮▮.

own lives? It seems as if they will. The Koko Maya framework contains powerful themes such as the struggle against manufactured food, the conflict between popular culture and family goals, the fight against conformity, and the problem of creating whole lives in a fragmented world.

It offers various mechanisms for addressing these themes, such as healthier alternatives, positive family rituals, glimpses of a different culture, and community involvement.

It teems with symbols, including the social power of tea, the love-inducing properties of chocolate, the exotic history of the Mayans, and the mischievous nature of monkeys.

All that's needed to bring this story to life is a hero: the customer.

Or course, every story has an arc. In branding, the arc is the customer's journey from a first awareness of the product to, in the best outcome, an authentic commitment to the brand. When the arcs of all the customers are taken together, they add up to an overall arc.

All we need now is a way to measure progress.

In the pre-flip days of marketing, the important number to watch was sales. Not just current sales, but projected sales, which you could estimate by tracking customers as they moved from awareness to interest to consideration to intent to evaluation and, finally, to purchase. Over time, you could see that a certain percentage of people from each stage would move to the next, until a very small percentage would drop into the bucket as sales.

This model of measurement, called the PURCHASE FUNNEL, is only helpful if 1) your main goal is to project sales in the short term, 2) customers move toward their purchase in predictable stages, 3) current revenues are more important than brand-building, 4) acquiring customers is more important than keeping them, 5) or you have no use for non-customers. There are a lot of ifs here, most of which no longer pan out.

For example, in a time of accelerating change, short-term revenues don't predict long-term or even medium-term success.

Furthermore, customers no longer purchase in predictable stages. On today's e-commerce

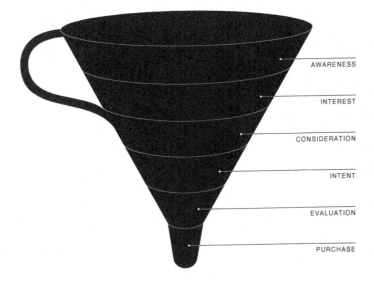

AWARENESS

INTEREST

CONSIDERATION

INTENT

EVALUATION

PURCHASE

PURCHASE FUNNEL

websites, all the stages of the sales funnel can reside in the same place: you can see a product for the first time, consider it, read customer comments, and make your purchase—all without leaving the site. To the customer, there is no funnel. The path from awareness to purchase is nonlinear and immediate.

The funnel image is wrong from a company perspective, too. Instead of stuffing people into a funnel to squeeze out profits, companies should be empowering customers so they can help build the brand. This is not to say that monthly and quarterly revenues are not important. Just that monthly and quarterly revenues are more sizable, more profitable, and more dependable when you focus on long-term relationships instead of short-term revenues.

Marketers need to set aside the funnel and pick up the ladder. The Brand Commitment Scale (BCS), or customer ladder, is a simple tool for measuring the progress of a brand from customer satisfaction to customer empowerment. The BCS puts the emphasis where it belongs—on the customer. It offers a clear metric as to how a company is doing at each level. The object is to get as many customers as possible up the ladder to the top.

Here's how it works. The bottom rung represents

customer satisfaction. This is where trust begins. The customer has tried your product or service and found it to be as advertised. This may be a function of selling a good product, or setting modest expectations, or both. The J. D. Powers surveys are well-known examples of this metric. While satisfaction is a good sign, studies have shown that satisfaction alone is not a reliable predictor of repurchase behavior or customer loyalty.

The next rung up is customer delight. Here's where trust really catches fire. If you can surprise your customer with something more than baseline satisfaction, you'll spark the kind of emotion that leads to loyalty. This is the realm of great customer experience. Forrester Research measures delight with its Customer Experience Index, and so does Bain & Company with its Net Promoter Score. Delight is the leading cause of a customer's "willingness to recommend."

One level higher is customer engagement. When a customer is truly engaged with a brand, he or she enrolls in the tribe. With membership comes increasing loyalty, escalating repurchase habits, and an emotional attachment that goes far beyond patronage. This is where the brand becomes a building block in the customer's identity, success, well-being, and even fulfillment. Havas's Meaningful Brands Index (MBi) has shown that top brands in this metric outperform the stock market by 120 percent.

On the top rung is customer empowerment. This is the level at which customers incorporate your brand into the deepest part of their lives. They may depend on it for emotional support, social status, personal growth, or even business success. They would no more switch to another brand than swap their right leg for a wooden peg. If you suddenly pulled your brand out from under them, they would collapse in a heap.

Empowered customers will move heaven and earth to ensure your success, happily attracting others to the tribe with their magnetic sense of commitment. One measure of this commitment is the Stengel 50. Developed by former P&G marketer Jim Stengel along with Millward Brown Optimor, it's a list of 50 brands with the deepest customer relationships. A 10-year investment in these brands would have generated 400 percent higher returns than the S&P 500.

The Brand Commitment Scale is an easy-to-use

EMPOWERMENT — PERSONAL GROWTH / EMOTIONAL SUPPORT / BUSINESS SUCCESS / SOCIAL STATUS / FULFILLMENT

ENGAGEMENT — TRIBAL ENROLLMENT / CUSTOMER LOYALTY / AUTOMATIC REPURCHASE / EMOTIONAL ATTACHMENT / SENSE OF BELONGING

DELIGHT — SURPRISE / PEAK EXPERIENCE / SOCIAL RECOMMENDATIONS / EXCITEMENT / INCREASING TRUST

SATISFACTION — FAIRNESS / BEGINNING OF TRUST / WILLING TO REPURCHASE / SENSE OF CLOSURE / CONFIDENCE

BRAND COMMITMENT SCALE

BRAND COMMITMENT SCALE (BCS) SURVEY

SATISFIED Grade each from 1–5.

_____ The company/product has met my expectations.

_____ The company charges a fair price for its product.

_____ **TOTAL** (highest score 10)

DELIGHTED Grade each from 1–5. Multiply total by 2.

_____ I've been pleasantly surprised by the company/product.

_____ I would happily recommend it to others.

_____ **TOTAL × 2** (highest score 20)

ENGAGED Grade each from 1–5. Multiply total by 3.

_____ I identify well with other customers of this company/product.

_____ I would go out of my way for the company and its customers.

_____ **TOTAL × 3** (highest score 30)

EMPOWERED Grade each from 1–5. Multiply total by 4.

_____ The company/product is essential to my life.

_____ I would be very sorry if it went out of business.

_____ **TOTAL × 4** (highest score 40)

_____ **GRAND TOTAL = BCS** (highest score 100)

survey that yields a single number from 20–100. This score represents your overall progress up the brand ladder, where empowerment is given four times the weight of satisfaction. If conducted annually, the BCS can highlight your gains (or losses), suggesting where you need more investment. It can also let you compare the scores at each rung of the ladder, and for each of the eight questions.

The power of this survey lies in its simplicity. All it takes is a service like Zoomerang or Survey-Monkey and a little of your customers' time. A sample of 1,000 surveys should be enough for most companies to get a useful reading.

Using the brand ladder, let's imagine the progress of Lori's brand over five years. From the very start, Koko Maya was a critical success. The product and its presentation were good enough to deliver more than satisfaction. It made a strong showing in customer delight, the second rung of the ladder.

In the first year, Lori introduced website features such as What's Cooking (tips and recipes for moms) and Koko's Korner (puzzles and projects for kids), which became popular forums for a wide range of conversations. Two years later she developed a successful model for putting on school fundraisers, giving moms a clear role in community involvement. In the meantime, revenues from the website and retailers had climbed to $15 million, and customers had climbed to the third rung of the brand ladder.

The company made steady gains over the next two years, bringing Lori to national attention through major articles in FAST COMPANY, FORBES, and VOGUE. The BBC then made a short documentary on the company and aired it worldwide. Riding this wave of public attention, she was able to persuade the Girl Scouts to retire their calorie-filled cookies in favor of Koko Maya Tea Biscuits. Profits grew 50 percent that year, validating the move and sending Koko Maya's brand to new heights.

The company then began training "certified tea caterers," customers who could host in-home tea parties. They became independent business owners, taking on gigs as their schedules permitted. A new army of empowered customers moved the brand up to the fourth rung of the ladder.

During the following decade, the company grew at a much faster rate than expected, thanks to a committed tribe of customers. Lori wrote a memoir, called THE MONKEY TREE, which was named "best business book of the year" by Amazon. She had

been spending more and more time in Guatemala,
a country she had come to love. Finally, after 15
years in the business she decided to retire there.

That same year the company generated more
than $1.5 billion in sales. It counted more than
two million people as customers. It supported 3,600
employees and freelance caterers. And it touched
families in 47 countries around the world. Not bad
for a "nothing" little product like tea.

While Lori's story is made up, it demonstrates
how companies can flip their brands into a new
state—one that generates more value by handing
more control to customers. It questions the belief
that business is a zero-sum game in which customers must lose so the company can win. And it
shows that the brand is only as strong as its tribe.

Of course, brands are only a small part of
our lives. We care much more about our families,
friends, pets, neighborhoods, careers, health, and
just having a good time. But that doesn't mean a
brand can't play a powerful, profitable role in these
things. You just need to flip your thinking: A brand
isn't what YOU say it is; it's what THEY say it is.

And what THEY say can make all the difference.

TAKE-HOME LESSONS

→ An explosion of connectivity, and the power it gives customers, is turning companies upside down.

→ Industry is undergoing a massive migration from a material-based economy to a digital one.

→ The question isn't WHETHER your company will be disrupted, but WHEN.

→ Customers today don't "consume." HAVING more runs a distant second to BEING more.

→ Today's customers want more than features, more than benefits, and more than experiences. They want MEANING.

→ They don't BUY brands. They JOIN brands. They want a vote in what gets produced and how it gets delivered.

→ A successful brand can become a touchstone in a customer's life—a vivid symbol of what's useful, delightful, and even magical.

→ When a product becomes a symbol, the symbol becomes the product.

→ In a flipped business, the product is not the innovation, the customer is. The company with the best customers wins.

→ The best brand builders see greatness in their customers, and figure out ways to enable it.

→ Any effort to get customers is marketing. Any effort to KEEP THEM is branding.

→ The best question to ask a new product marketer is not "How big is the segment," but "You and what army?"

→ In the age of easy group-forming, the basic unit of measurement is not the segment but the TRIBE.

→ To achieve authenticity with your tribe, you have to begin with company purpose—the reason you're in business beyond making money.

→ Each brand experience should be the brand in miniature, a representative sample of what your customers understand about the company and its offerings.

→ You can't DECIDE a great customer experience. You have to DESIGN it.

→ Delight in the minimal, the ultra clear, the super simple. Never add without trying to subtract.

→ The goal of designing prototypes is not to impress your customers, but let them impress YOU with their reactions, knowledge, and insights.

→ We now live in a world of participatory theater in which we watch the performance and simultaneously judge the performer.

→ Customers don't want to be TOLD, they want to TELL. They long to be the heroes of their own journey.

→ Empowered customers will move heaven and earth to ensure your success, happily attracting others to the tribe with their magnetic sense of commitment.

→ A brand isn't what YOU say it is. It's what THEY say it is.

THE BRAND GAP, Marty Neumeier (New Riders, 2003). This, my first book on branding, shows companies how to bridge the gap between business strategy and customer experience. It defines brand-building as a system that includes five disciplines: differentiation, collaboration, innovation, validation, and cultivation. Like **THE BRAND FLIP** and **ZAG**, it was designed as "whiteboard overview"—a two-hour read that can also serve as a reference tool.

DECODING THE NEW CONSUMER MIND, Kit Yarrow (Jossey-Bass, 2014). Marketing psychologist Kit Yarrow explains how technology has rewired our brains, making us more individualistic, isolated, emotional, and distrustful. This is not a pessimistic book—it's a practical guide to addressing customers' desires and insecurities in a time of deep cultural shifts. Not only has she done her homework, she presents the results with lightness and clarity.

THE DESIGNFUL COMPANY, Marty Neumeier (New Riders, 2009). Forget total quality. Forget top-down strategy. In an era of fast-moving markets and leap-frogging innovation, we can no longer decide the way forward. We now have to design the way forward. The third book in my whiteboard series shows leaders and managers how to transform the organization into a powerhouse of brand innovation.

A SMILE IN THE MIND, Beryl McAlhone and David Stuart (Phaidon, 1998). If you buy only one book on graphic design, make it this one. Designer Stuart and writer McAlhone prove that wit is the soul of innovation, using clever and often profound examples from American and European designers, plus a few pieces from Stuart's own firm, The Partners, in London. Look for the new 2016 edition.

TILT, Niraj Dawar (Harvard Business Review Press, 2013). This book by a professor of marketing at the Ivey Business School makes many of the same points as **THE BRAND FLIP**, but from a traditional business perspective. His clearly made argument is that strategic advantage is shifting from upstream activities like product manufacturing to downstream activities like brand building.

TRIBES, Seth Godin (Portfolio, 2008). More manifesto than business book, **TRIBES** puts out a passionate call for leaders in the age of easy group-forming. "The Web can do many things," says Godin, "but it can't provide leadership." Tribes emerge when people are connected to each other, to a leader, and to an idea that matters. To the extent that brands are movements, they need great leaders.

WHO DO YOU WANT YOUR CUSTOMERS TO BECOME? Michael Schrage (Harvard Business Review Press, 2012). It's a startling question, especially to companies that focus on their own success instead of the success of their customers. But if you're out to build a lasting brand, it's the right question to ask. Schrage shows why the goal of innovation should not be to invent a great product but to create a great customer.

ZAG, Marty Neumeier (New Riders, 2007). Whereas **THE BRAND GAP** outlines the five disciplines needed to build a charismatic brand, **ZAG** drills down into the first of the disciplines, differentiation. In an age of me-too products and instant communications, winning companies are those that can out-position, out-maneuver, and out-design the competition. The rule? When everybody zigs, zag.

ACKNOWLEDGMENTS   The trick to writing a short book is to take a long book and squeeze the air out of it. I take secret delight in seeing one of my books with highlights, underlines, and notes on every page.

I couldn't achieve this without the help of many, many people. Some of them I've never met except through books, and others I've had the pleasure of working with side by side. I've grown richer with each experience.

Among these experiences are many happy encounters with the people of Liquid Agency, where I've worked for the last six years. My thanks go to Scott Gardner, co-founder and CEO; Alfredo Muccino, co-founder and chief creative officer; Dennis Hahn, chief strategy officer; Katie Wagner, director of client services in our Portland office; Hunter Marshall, director of strategy in our Portland office; Martha Bowman, director of strategy in our San Jose office; Tony Cordero, creative director in our San Francisco office; and Lisa Peyton, a friend of the agency. Together they helped me work through the imaginary case study of Koko Maya, using the Brand Commitment process that I outline in the book.

Thanks also to my early readers, who offered encouragement at various stages of the process. These included Nancy Dillon, a good friend and former editor who read the book with a kind and critical eye; Niraj Dawar, author and marketing professor at the Ivey Business School; Ric Grefé, executive director of AIGA, the professional association for design; Robert Jones, brand strategist at Wolff Olins in London, and professor at the University of East Anglia; Greg Petroff, chief experience officer at GE; Michael Schrage, author of insightful books on creative collaboration (you should read them); John Spence, business guru and author of books on leadership; Kit Yarrow, Ph.D., author and professor of consumer psychology; and Doru Bere, founder of Dreambox. I'm grateful to all for taking time from their busy schedules.

A book is only a lifeless manuscript unless it's designed, illustrated, and crafted as an experience. I'm indebted to Irene Hoffman, who not only helped design and produce the books, but cast a critical eye over the typography, layout, pacing, and continuity of the text. She brought an author's sensibility to the flow of ideas, and caught many logical errors that would have normally slipped by.

Special thanks to Cya Nelson for giving freely of her talents and designing the final Koko Maya package. A bow to Anthony Smith, British designer who surrendered part of his American vacation to lend me his advice and drawing skills. (He's the one who inked those amazing monkeys.) My appreciation also goes to photographer Jay Farbman, model Melinda Greene, and designers Jenny Lee and Brooke Klass for their various contributions.

Finally, a book is not a book until a publisher prints and distributes it. My continuing thanks to Peachpit's former publisher Nancy Aldrich-Ruenzel, who has stuck with me and sometimes challenged me over the course of six books and related products. I'm grateful for the guidance of editor Nikki McDonald, who led me safely past the pitfalls of titling, cover design, and legal omissions. It was a pleasure—as always—to work with David Van Ness, whose kind attention during the production phase makes every project easier. Thanks once again to Liz Welch, a master proofreader; Rebecca Plunkett for the index; and Lupe Edgar for being a constant advocate and manager of great ebook design.

I've saved the most important acknowledgment for last. My wife Eileen is the person I most try to please with my work. She allows me to borrow from her library of literary knowledge, as well as her wisdom about subjects beyond business. While she may not have taught me how to write, she continually inspires me to listen, learn, and appreciate the highest achievements of culture and the arts. Here's lookin' at you, kid.

INDEX

A

ACADEMY OF MARKETING SCIENCE, **70**

ADVERTISING
FOCUSING ON CUSTOMER
EXPERIENCE VS., **54**
INAUTHENTIC MESSAGES IN, **53**
SEE ALSO **BRANDS**

AERON, **60**

AIMS (BRAND COMMITMENT MATRIX),
46–47, 48, 49, 67

AIRBNB, **35**

AMAZON, **2–3, 54, 69**

ANTHROPOLOGIE, **54**

APPLE, **35, 36, 52, 54, 69, 93**

AUTHENTICITY SCORECARD, **55**

AUTHORITY VS. AUTHENTICITY, **51–56**

AXA, **77, 78**

B

BAIN & COMPANY'S NET PROMOTER
SCORE, **123**

BATTLE BETWEEN TRIBES, **13**

BEING VS. HAVING, **3, 131**

BELONGING, **20**

BEZOS, JEFF, **101**

BLOCKBUSTER VIDEO, **78**

BMW, **106**

BRANCHING, **106–110**

BRAND ASSET VALUATOR, **83**

BRAND COMMITMENT MATRIX
AS CUSTOMER LADDER, **122–125**
DESIGNING LIQUID BRANDS USING, **111–113**
EXAMPLE OF, **66, 67**
HOW IT WORKS, **46–49**
SURVEY FOR, **126**

BRAND COMMITMENT SCALE (BCS)
SURVEY, **122, 124, 126–127**

BRAND EXPERIENCE MAP
DEVELOPING, **86–87, 90**
TOUCHPOINTS ON, **71, 73–75**

BRAND EXTENSIONS, **102**

BRAND GAP, THE (NEUMEIER), **1–2, 134**

BRAND LADDER, **122–125**

BRANDS
BRANCHING OF, **106–110**

CHANGING FOCUS IN, **2**

CUSTOMERS' OWNERSHIP OF, **5**

DEFINING, **20–23, 27**

DESIGNING CUSTOMER IDENTITIES
WITH, **32–35**

FLOW THROUGH MULTIPLE
TECHNOLOGIES, **16**

JOINING, **6, 29, 131**

MATRIX FOR, **46–49, 66, 67**

MEASURING COMMITMENT TO, **124, 126–127**

MOVING TO CUSTOMER PROTECTION, **77–83**

OLD AND NEW MODELS OF, **3–5**

PROTOTYPING DESIGNS FOR, **92–99, 103**

PROVIDING CUSTOMER EXPERIENCES,
70–71, 85–91

SIMPLICITY IN, **100–103, 133**

STATIC VS. LIQUID, **104–113**

STORY ARC IN, **229**

SUCCESS OF FLUID, **17**

TAKE-HOME LESSONS FOR, **131–133**

TOUCHPOINTS FOR, **68–76**

TRIBE SUPPORT FOR, **42**

WORST-PERFORMING, **77**

BRIN, SERGEY, **101**

BUNRAKU, **114, 115**

BUSINESSES. SEE **COMPANIES**

C

CAVEAT VENDITOR, **83**

CHESTERTON, G. K., **103**

CHEVRON, **53**

CIRQUE DU SOLEIL, **52, 60**

COCA COLA, **52**

COGNITIVE OVERHEAD, **101**

COMPANIES
AVOIDING COMPETITION, **58, 61**
CULTURES COMPATIBLE WITH TRIBES,
63, 65–66
CUSTOMER IDENTITY AND PURPOSE OF,
52–53
CUSTOMER LEADERSHIP IN, **6**
CUSTOMERS OF WINNING, **14, 132**
DESIGN-CENTRIC, **91**
DESIGNING CUSTOMER EXPERIENCES,
85–91

DEVELOPING TRIBE SUPPORT, 43–45
DIFFERENTIATING PRODUCTS, 59–61
ESTABLISHING AUTHENTICITY, 51–56
FINDING PRODUCT ONLYNESS, 57–61
FLIPPING ACCEPTED BUSINESS TRUTHS, 6
FOCUSING ON CUSTOMER IDENTITY, 32–33
MEASURING SALES WITH PURCHASE
    FUNNEL, 120, 121–122
MULTIPLYING AND CONQUERING, 40–45
NEW REALITIES FOR, 8–17
POV ACRONYM FOR, 47, 67
POWER SHIFT TO CUSTOMERS FROM, 8
PREPARING FOR DISRUPTION, 3, 131
PRODUCT-DRIVEN MODEL FOR, 5
PROTECTING CUSTOMERS, 77–83
RANKING AUTHENTICITY OF, 55
RETAINING CUSTOMERS, 30, 31
SOLVING SERVICE ISSUES, 82
STRENGTHENING TRIBES, 14
TAKE-HOME LESSONS FOR, 131
TESTING BRAND PROTOTYPES, 94
VALUE ADDED WITH INTANGIBLES, 26
COMPETITION
AVOIDING, 58, 61
COMPANIES WITH STRONGEST
    TRIBE WINS,14, 132
DIFFERENTIATING VS., 57–61
CONLEY, CHIP, 35, 54
CORPORATE CULTURE, 63, 65–66
CORPORATIONS. SEE **COMPANIES**
COSTS
OF LOGOS, 23
PROTOTYPING, 93
CREATIVE SWARM, 86
CSIKSZENTMIHALYI, MIHALY, 35
CUSTOMER EXPERIENCE
ADVERTISING VS., 54
BRANDS PROVIDING, 70–71, 85–91
CHOOSING GIFTS FOR, 24
CUSTOMER EXPERIENCE INDEX, 76
DESIGNING, 85–91
DRAWING TOUCHPOINTS FROM, 68
IMPROVING FOR CUSTOMER CALLS, 69–70
MEASURING, 123
USING SOCIAL MEDIA, 73–74

CUSTOMER EXPERIENCE INDEX, 76, 123
CUSTOMER SERVICE
CUSTOMER CALL CENTERS, 69–70
80/80 RULE FOR, 79–80
FINDING ISSUES TO FIX IN, 82
ZAPPOS'S COMMITMENT TO, 54
CUSTOMERS
ALIGNING PURPOSE TO, 52–53
BUILDING IDENTITIES WITH PRODUCTS, 10
BUYING IN TRIBES, 12
CO-LEADING COMPANIES, 6
CREATING OWN NARRATIVES, 116–117
DELIGHT OF, 123, 125, 126, 133
DESIGNING IDENTITIES OF, 32–35
EMPOWERING, 124, 125, 126, 133
FOCUSED ON MEANING, 9, 131
HATE BEING SOLD, LOVE BUYING, 11
IAM ACRONYM FOR, 46–47, 67
JOINING BRANDS, 6, 29, 131
LOYALTY OF, 29–31
MAKING PURCHASING DECISIONS, 80
MARKETING TO TRIBES OF, 40–45
MEASURING SATISFACTION OF,
    122–123, 125, 126
OWNERSHIP OF BRANDS, 5
POWER SHIFT TO, 8, 22–23, 35
PRIMACY OF, 1, 2–3
PRODUCTS IMPROVING AND
    POSITIONING, 36–39
PROVIDING SERVICE TO, 69–70
RETENTION OF, 30, 31
SURVEYING BRAND COMMITMENT OF,
    124, 126–127
TAKE-HOME LESSONS ABOUT, 131–133
TESTING PROTOTYPES WITH, 94
VIEWING AS FRIENDS, 54
SEE ALSO **CUSTOMER SERVICE**

D

DAWAR, NIRAJ, 57, 135
DECODING THE CONSUMER MIND
    (YARROW), 56, 134
DELIGHT OF CUSTOMERS, 123, 125, 126, 133
DELL, 37
DESIGN MANAGEMENT INSTITUTE, 91

DESIGNERS, **85–86**

DESIGNFUL MIND, THE (NEUMEIER), **134**

DESIGNING

   CUSTOMER EXPERIENCES, **85–91, 132**

   CUSTOMER IDENTITIES, **32–35**

   EXPERIMENTING WITH PROTOTYPES, **92–99**

   FORGIVENESS INTO WEBSITES, **81**

   WITH SIMPLICITY, **100–103, 133**

DISNEY, **60**

DISRUPTION OF COMPANIES, **3, 131**

DRUCKER, PETER, **1, 30, 33**

E

80/80 RULE, **79–80**

EMPOWERMENT OF CUSTOMERS,
   124, 125, 126, 133

ENEMIES OF SIMPLICITY, **102**

ENGAGEMENT OF CUSTOMERS,
   123–124, 125, 126

EXPERIENCES

   DRAWING TOUCHPOINTS FROM, **68**

   GIFT CARDS AND SHOPPING, **24**

   IMPROVING FOR CUSTOMER CALLS, **69–70**

EXTERNAL PROPS FOR IDENTITIES, **35**

F

FIT, **52–53**

FLIPPING

   ACCEPTED BUSINESS TRUTHS, **6**

   AUTHORITY TO AUTHENTICITY, **51–56**

   BRAND TO CUSTOMER PROTECTION,
      77–83

   FROM COMPETING TO
      DIFFERENTIATING, **57–61**

   TO CUSTOMER-CENTRIC MARKETPLACE,
      32–35

   DECIDING INTO DESIGNING, **85–91**

   FEATURES INTO EXPERIENCES, **68–76**

   MARKETING FROM PRODUCTS TO
      MEANING, **19–23**

   OVERCHOICE TO SIMPLICITY, **100–103, 133**

   PLANNING INTO EXPERIMENTS, **92–99**

   PROCESSES TO VALUES, **62–66**

   PRODUCT IMPROVEMENT TO BETTER
      CUSTOMERS, **36–39**

   PURCHASE FUNNEL TO BRAND LADDER,
      120–129

   SEGMENTS TO TRIBES, **40–45**

   FROM SELLING TO ENROLLING, **28–31**

   STATIC TO LIQUID BRANDS, **104–113**

   STORYTELLING TO STORYFRAMING, **114–119**

   SUMMARY OF, **131–133**

   FROM TANGIBLE TO IMMATERIAL
      PRODUCTS, **24–27**

   TRANSACTIONS TO RELATIONSHIPS, **46–49**

FLUID VS. STATIC BRANDS, **17**

FORGIVENESS, **81**

FORRESTER RESEARCH'S CUSTOMER
   EXPERIENCE INDEX, **76, 123**

G

GARDNER, JOHN, **117**

GARDNER, SCOTT, **105**

GODIN, SETH, **42, 54, 135**

GOOGLE, **35, 52, 101**

H

HASTINGS, REED, **81**

HAVAS'S MEANINGFUL BRANDS INDEX
   (MBI), **124**

I

IAM ACRONYM

   COMPONENTS OF, **46–47**

   EXAMPLE OF, **67**

   INCLUDING IN STORYFRAMING, **117**

IBM, **36**

IDENTITIES

   BUILDING CUSTOMER, **10**

   COMPANY VS. CUSTOMER, **32–35**

   EXTERNAL PROPS FOR, **35**

IDENTITY (BRAND COMMITMENT
   MATRIX), **46–48, 49, 67**

IKEA, **54**

IMPRESSION OF PRODUCTS AS BRANDS, **21**

INNOVATOR'S HYPOTHESIS
   (SCHRAGE), **92–93**

INTANGIBLES

   ADDING VALUE WITH, **26**

   GROWING VALUE OF, **25**

J

J. D. POWERS, 123
JOBS, STEVE, 35, 36, 86, 93
JOHNSON & JOHNSON, 63, 65
JOIE DE VIVRE, 35, 54
JOINING BRANDS, 6, 29, 131

K

KELLY, KEVIN, 25

L

LIQUID AGENCY, 24, 105
LIQUID BRANDS
  BRANCHING BY, 106–110
  CHARACTERISTICS OF, 104–108
  EXAMPLE OF, 110–113
LOGOS
  BRAND VS., 21
  COSTS OF, 23
LOWE, NICK, 93
LOWRY, ADAM, 65

M

MADONNA, 51–52
MARKETING
  COLLAPSE OF NARRATIVE IN, 116
  FINDING CUSTOMER TRIBES FOR, 40–45
  MAKING SELLING SUPERFLUOUS, 29, 30
  FOR MEANING, 20, 131
  TRENDS FOR PRODUCTS, 19–20
  SEE ALSO **BRANDS**
MARTIN, RYAN, 80
MCALHONE, BERYL, 134
MEANING
  ADDING TO PRODUCTS, 56
  MARKETING PRODUCTS FOR, 20, 131
  PEOPLE'S FOCUS ON, 9, 131
MEANINGFUL BRANDS INDEX (MBI), 124
MEASURING
  BRAND COMMITMENT, 122, 124, 126–127
  CUSTOMER SATISFACTION,
    122–123, 125, 126
  DELIGHT, 123, 125, 126
  EMPOWERMENT OF CUSTOMERS,
    124, 125, 126

ENGAGEMENT OF CUSTOMERS,
  123–124, 125, 126
  POWER OF LOYALTY, 29–31
  SALES WITH PURCHASE FUNNEL,
    120, 121–122
METHOD, 65, 69, 70
MILLWARD BROWN OPTIMOR, 124
MINI USA, 35, 91
MOM BLOGGER TRIBE, 43–45
MONETARY VALUE OF INTANGIBLES, 25, 27
MORES (BRAND COMMITMENT MATRIX),
  47, 48, 49
MOTIV STRATEGIES, 91
MUCCINO, ALFREDO, 24
MULTIPLYING MARKETS, 40–45

N

NET PROMOTER SCORE, 123
NETFLIX, 78, 79, 81
NEUMEIER, MARTY, 1–2, 134, 135
NORDSTROM, 69

O

O'LEARY, MICHAEL, 77
ONLYNESS, 57, 58, 59–61, 67
OVERCHOICE, 100–103

P

P&G, 38
PACQUET, SÉBASTIEN, 41
PAGE, LARRY, 35, 101
PAYPAL, 58
PEOPLE. SEE **CUSTOMERS**
PLANNING, 92
POSTREL, VIRGINIA, 53
POUR YOUR HEART INTO IT (SCHULTZ), 73
POV ACRONYM
  DESIGNING FOR NEW BRAND, 113
  EXAMPLE OF, 67
  INCLUDING IN STORYFRAMING, 117
  OUTLINING BRAND'S VISION WITH, 47, 67
POWER
  FOUND IN IMMATERIAL VALUES, 25
  OF LOYALTY, 29–31
  SHIFT TO CUSTOMERS, 8, 22–23, 35

POWERSHIFT (TOFFLER), **25**
PRACTICE OF MANAGEMENT, THE
    (DRUCKER), **1**
PRESENT SHOCK (RUSHKOFF), **114**
PRESS, JIM, **65**
PROCESSES VS. VALUES, **62–66**
PRODUCT-DRIVEN COMPANY MODEL, **5**
PRODUCTS
    BRANDS VS., **21**
    BUILDING IDENTITIES WITH, **10**
    DIFFERENTIATING, **59–61**
    IMPROVING AND POSITIONING
        CUSTOMERS WITH, **36–39**
    MARKETING TRENDS FOR, **19–20**
    AS SYMBOLS, **27**
    TANGIBLE VS. IMMATERIAL, **24–27**
PROFIT AND CUSTOMER RETENTION, **30, 31**
PROFLUENCE, **117**
PROGRESSIVE, **81**
PROMISES AS BRAND, **21–22**
PROTOTYPING, **92–99, 103**
PURCHASE FUNNEL, **120, 121–122**
PURPLE COW (GODIN), **54**
PURPOSE
    ALIGNING TO CUSTOMER IDENTITY, **52–53**
    ON BRAND COMMITMENT MATRIX, **67**

R
RAGE OF STRANGERS, **80, 83**
RECOMMENDED READING, **134–135**
REGF (RIDICULOUSLY EASY
    GROUP-FORMING), **40–41**
RELATIONSHIPS
    BRANDS VS., **22**
    CONVERTING TRANSACTIONS TO,
        46–49
REPUTATION VS. BRANDS, **22**
RESTORATION HARDWARE, **100**
RETENTION OF CUSTOMERS, **30, 31**
RIDICULOUSLY EASY GROUP-FORMING
    (REGF), **40–41**
RITZ-CARLTON, **37, 63, 64, 68–69, 83**
RUSHKOFF, DOUGLAS, **114, 116**
RYAN, ERIC, **65**
RYANAIR, **77–79**

S
SALES
    CUSTOMER PURCHASING AS TRIBES, **12**
    ENROLLING VS. SELLING, **28–31**
    MEASURING WITH PURCHASE FUNNEL,
        120, 121–122
    NEW REALITIES FOR, **11**
    AS TRANSACTIONS, **46**
SATISFACTION OF CUSTOMERS,
    122–123, 125, 126
SCHRAGE, MICHAEL, **37, 92–93, 135**
SCHULTZ, HOWARD, **73**
SEGMENTATION, **40**
SENK, GLEN, **54**
SERVICE VALUES, **63, 64**
SHIPPING, **74**
SHIRKY, CLAY, **100–101**
SIEGEL+GALE, **77**
SIMPLICITY, **100–103, 133**
SMILE IN THE MIND, A
    (MCALHONE AND STUART), **134**
SOCIAL MEDIA
    DESIGNING EXPERIENCES FOR, **73–74**
    MULTIPLYING MARKETS WITH, **40–41**
    RAGE ON, **80**
SOUTHWEST, **78–79**
STARBUCKS, **54**
STATIC VS. FLUID BRANDS, **17**
STENGEL **50, 124**
STENGEL, JIM, **124**
STORYTELLING VS. STORYFRAMING, **114–119**
STUART, DAVID, **134**
SYMBOLS, PRODUCTS AS, **27, 131**
SZKUTAK, TOM, **2**

T
T-MOBILE, **78, 79**
TAKE-HOME LESSONS, **131–133**
TANGIBLES, **27**
TECHNOLOGY
    BRAND FLOW THROUGH MULTIPLE, **16**
    CONNECTING TRIBES, **15**
    SEE ALSO **SOCIAL MEDIA; WEBSITES**
TEN NEW REALITIES, **8–17**
TESTING PROTOTYPES WITH CUSTOMERS, **94**

THEIL, PETER, 58
TILT (DAWAR), 57, 135
TOFFLER, ALVIN, 25
TOMS, 60
TOUCHPOINTS
  ABOUT, 68–76, 131
  ARRANGING ON BRAND EXPERIENCE
    MAP, 71, 73–75
  MENU OF, 72
TOYODA, AKIO, 30
TOYOTA, 30, 65
TRIBES
  ACHIEVING AUTHENTICITY WITH, 51–56
  BATTLE BETWEEN, 13
  BRANDS STRENGTHENED BY, 42
  BUYING IN, 12
  COMPANY CULTURES COMPATIBLE WITH,
    63, 65–66
  CONNECTIONS AMONG, 15
  DEFINED, 41
  MARKETING TO, 40–45
  WINNING COMPANIES HAVE STRONGEST,
    14, 132
TRIBES (GODIN), 42, 135
TWITTER, 60

U
UBER, 24
U.S. EXPORTS, 25

V
VALUES
  ADDING WITH INTANGIBLES, 26
  ON BRAND COMMITMENT MATRIX, 67
  FLIPPING COMPANY PROCESSES TO, 62–66
  RITZ-CARLTON SERVICE, 63, 64
  SHAPING COMPANY CULTURE WITH, 63, 64
VIRGIN, 60
VIRTUOUS CIRCLE OF IMPROVEMENT, 69–70
VOLVO, 58

W
WATERMARK CONSULTING, 76
WEBSITES
  AVOIDING CLUTTER ON, 101, 103

  FORGIVENESS DESIGNED INTO, 81
  UNCOVERING IRRITATIONS ON, 80–81
WEIGEL, MARTIN, 105
WHAT TECHNOLOGY WANTS (KELLY), 25
WHO DO YOU WANT YOUR CUSTOMERS TO
  BECOME (SCHRAGE), 37, 135
WHOLE FOODS, 54
WORLD OF PARTICIPATORY THEATRE,
  114, 115, 133

Y
Y&R, 83
YARROW, KIT, 56, 80, 83, 134

Z
ZAG (NEUMEIER), 1, 2, 135
ZAPPOS, 54, 56, 69
ZIPCAR, 24

NOTES   PAGE 2   Szkutak quote: "How Amazon Trained Its Investors to Behave," by Justin Fox, *HBR*, January 30, 2013.

24   Muccino quote: "The Future of Retail," Alfredo Muccino and Emily Buccholtz, Liquid Agency website, http://www.liquidagency.com/brand-exchange/retail-is-dating/

25   A recent study of the S&P 500: "4 Key Reasons Why Branding Is Important," by Melissa Mazzoleni, *HOW*, December 4, 2014.

30   Drucker quote: *Management*, by Peter F. Drucker (HarperBusiness, 1973).

37   Ritz motto: www.ritzcarlton.com/en/corporate/goldstandards/

37   Dell purpose: www.dell.com/learn/us/en/uscorp1/purpose-and-values

38   P&G purpose: www.pg.com/translations/pvp_pdf/english_PVP.pdf

68   Ritz-Carlton credo: www.ritzcarlton.com/en/corporate/goldstandards

70   Transcendent customer experiences: "Transcendent customer experiences and brand community," by Schouten, McAlexander, and Koenig, *Journal of the Academy of Marketing Science*, May 9, 2007.

76   Forrester Research Customer Service Index: http://www.mycustomer. com/blogs-post/customer-experience-uk-and-beyond/167258

76   Customer service leaders outstrip the S&P 500: "The 2014 Customer Experience ROI Study," by Jon Picoult, www.watermarkconsult.net/blog

77   Siegel+Gale survey: http://www.siegelgale.com/media_mention/ ryanair-named-second-worst-brand-world-customer-service

80   Customers want five things: *Decoding the New Consumer Mind*, by Kit Yarrow (Jossey-Bass, 2014).

80   Ryan Martin, rage of strangers: "Clicking Their Way to Outrage," by Teddy Wayne, *The New York Times*, July 3, 2014.

81   Subscriber happiness: "A Resurgent Netflix Beats Projections, Even Its Own," by Brian Stelter, *The New York Times,* January 23, 2013

83   Y&R's Brand Asset Valuator: *Decoding the New Consumer Mind,* by Kit Yarrow (Jossey-Bass, 2014).

91   Return on design investment: http://www.dmi.org/?DesignValue

105   Martin Weigel quote: "Your Brand Is Software, Not a Person," by Martin Weigel, martinweigel.org, October 14, 2014.

124   Meaningful Brands Index: http://www.havasmedia.com/press /press-releases/2013/meaningful_brands_beat_stock_marke

125   Stengel 50: http://www.jimstengel.com/grow/research-valida

Marty Neumeier is Director of Transformation at Liquid Agency, a firm that develops brands for "fast companies"—organizations that depend on innovation, disruption, and relentless growth for success. This is his sixth book on brand building and business creativity.

His first book, **THE BRAND GAP**, redefined a brand as "a customer's gut feeling about a product, service, or organization," rejecting the widely held view that a brand was a logo or a campaign promise. His next book **ZAG**, introduced "onlyness" as the true test of a brand strategy, and was named one the "100 Best Business Books of All Time." His third book, **THE DESIGNFUL COMPANY**, offered leaders a blueprint for building a culture of brand innovation.

He joined Liquid Agency in a 2009 merger. Liquid offers clients a full range of services from brand planning and messaging to brand identity and experience design. Its presence in Silicon Valley gave it early access to the people, ideas, and companies that are now transforming the world. From this vantage point came "Silicon Valley thinking," an approach that informs the work of all its offices, from San Jose and San Francisco to Portland, New York, and Santiago.

In 2012 Neumeier published **METASKILLS**, a book about workplace creativity in an age of increasing automation. He followed **METASKILLS** with **THE 46 RULES OF GENIUS**, a "quickstart guide" to innovation mastery.

His vision for business creativity has led to engagements with many of industry's most exciting companies, including Apple, Google, Microsoft, Twitter, and Patagonia. From these experiences he has drawn the principles he shares in his books, keynotes, and workshops.

When Marty isn't advising clients or leading workshops, he retreats to the Aquitaine region of France, where he and his wife keep a *petite maison*. After nearly ten years of trying to speak French, he still confuses *pommes* with *pommes de terre*.